Issues in Second Language Teaching

To Bernadette

'Noi speriamo in un mondo che riesca a migliorare la qualità della vita di tutti, l'ambiente, la possibilità di conoscere, la possibilità di comunicare appunto e di informare, e soprattutto la possibilità di eliminare tutto quello che è oggetto per distruggersi, il fatto di poter far scomparire le armi, le guerre, la pena capitale. Ecco io credo, che già quello sarebbe un cambiamento enorme.'

Intervista a Gian Maria Volonte, 1994 (sul set del film *Lo sguardo di Ulisse*)

Issues in Second Language Teaching

Alessandro G. Benati

SHEFFIELD UK   BRISTOL CT

Published by Equinox Publishing Ltd.

UK: Kelham House, 3 Lancaster Street, Sheffield, S3 8AF
USA: ISD, 70 Enterprise Drive, Bristol, CT 06010

www.equinoxpub.com

First published 2013

Alessandro G. Benati

ISBN-13   978 1 84553 925 2   (hardback)
          978 1 84553 926 9   (paperback)

British Library Cataloguing-in-Publication Data

A catalogue record for this book is available from the British Library.

Library of Congress Cataloging-in-Publication Data

Benati, Alessandro G.
 Issues in second language teaching / Alessandro G. Benati.
    pages cm
 Includes bibliographical references and index.
 ISBN 978-1-84553-925-2 (hb) -- ISBN 978-1-84553-926-9 (pb)
 1. Language teachers--Training of. 2. Language and languages--Study and teaching.
 3. Second language acquisition. I. Title.
 P53.85.B47 2013
 418.0071--dc23
                          2012045138

Typeset by ISB Typesetting, Sheffield, UK

Printed and bound in Great Britain by Latimer Trend & Company Ltd., Plymouth

Contents

Acknowledgements

I would like to express my gratitude to all my students and my colleagues who have helped me over the years to develop a better understanding of how languages are learned and should be taught. A thank you to friends and colleagues who have read this book and provided important suggestions to improve its content and style. A special thank you to Tanja Angelovska for her advice and suggestions in the first draft of the book. Finally, I would like to say thank you to the two anonymous reviewers for their valuable comments.

A special thanks to my daughter Grace, my son Francesco, and my wife Bernadette to whom this book is dedicated.

Last but not least I would like to thank all the staff at Equinox for helping me during the development and the production of this volume.

Preface

Issues in Second Language Teaching is a book written in order to help trainee teachers and more experienced teachers reflect on certain topics and key issues related to second language teaching. Despite the proliferation of books and courses in language teaching methodologies, most of these courses and books focus on the description of specific methods and sometimes fail to emphasize the crucial interplay between how people learn languages and what it is the most effective way to teach languages.

The overall aim of this textbook is to reflect on certain key issues in second language teaching in order to provide readers and language instructors with a principled and evidence-based approach to language teaching. Knowing how languages are learned will help language instructors develop a more innovative and effective way to teach a language and to create the necessary conditions for learners to learn more efficiently and appropriately. We aim to develop and enhance readers' theoretical and practical understanding of how language instructors approach the way they teach languages in the classroom. An analysis of how the principles derived from research can be applied in the language classroom when it comes to issues such as teaching grammar, correcting errors, providing 'good' input and developing output activities which provide L2 learners with good opportunities for interaction, is the main purpose of this volume. More specifically the book will have the following aims:

1. To develop readers' awareness of the relationship between theory and practice in language learning and language teaching.
2. To develop readers' awareness of the theoretical and practical key issues related to the teaching of a second language.
3. To develop readers' abilities to analyse, reflect and evaluate specific techniques/tasks which have been proved to be appropriate and effective in language teaching when it comes to teaching grammar, providing corrective feedback, encouraging interaction in the language classroom, providing input- and output-based language tasks and developing different language skills.

Although in this book a traditional approach in language teaching (e.g. mechanical drills, translation tasks) is challenged, the present volume, designed for language teachers and students, does not support a particular methodology or technique, but provides an evidence-based approach to language teaching. Language instruction should ensure that learners:

- develop linguistic and communicative competence;
- engage with language tasks where meaning is emphasized over form. However, a focus on form is an essential component in second language learning and teaching;
- are exposed to extensive 'good quality' input. However, it is essential that learners are given opportunities for output practice;
- are exposed to language tasks where they have the opportunity to interact with each other, exchange information and negotiate meaning;
- engage in effective tasks (e.g. information-exchange tasks, discourse type tasks, role-playing, authentic materials);
- receive a minimum of error correction, and are encouraged to self-repair;
- have considerable exposure to the second language speech from the instructor and other learners, and instructors should provide opportunities for learners to play an active role during the language task;
- work in pairs or in groups during the completion of a language task. In group work learners are encouraged to negotiate meaning, use a variety of linguistic forms and functions;
- engage in language tasks which integrate their skills to reflect a more authentic use of language;
- are exposed to authentic materials so that they will be better prepared to deal with real language outside the classroom settings.

This book comprises an introduction and eight sections:

Chapter 1: Key Developments in Second Language Teaching

In this chapter, some of the key developments in terms of language methodologies over the last sixty years are briefly reviewed – from the Grammar Translation Method to the Communicative Language Teaching approach. Some guidelines to adopt the most effective approach in language teaching will be provided at the end of the chapter.

Chapter 2: Key Issues in Grammar Teaching

In this chapter, several approaches/techniques to grammar instruction are reviewed. From input-based options (e.g. processing instruction practice; input enhancement techniques) to structured-based options to grammar instruction (e.g. consciousness raising approach). Output-based options to grammar instruction such as collaborative output tasks are also examined. The chapter provides the reader with an opportunity to reflect on research and practices on the teaching of grammar and offers some overall guidelines and suggestions for language teachers.

Chapter 3: Key Issues in Interactional and Corrective Feedback

In this chapter, a number of different techniques to provide L2 learners with a focus on grammar through interactional and corrective feedback are examined. Key approaches to interaction and corrective feedback are based on the assumption that negotiated interaction is a key element in second language acquisition.

Chapter 4: Key Issues in the Teaching of Speaking

In this chapter, several ways in which speaking skills can be enhanced in the language classroom will be examined. General guidelines will be provided to develop an effective approach to the teaching of speaking.

Chapter 5: Key Issues in the Teaching of Listening

In this chapter, a number of ways in which listening skills can be enhanced in the language classroom will be presented. Principles will be provided as to how to develop effective tasks that help learners improve their listening skills.

Chapter 6: Key Issues in the Teaching of Reading

In this chapter, a pedagogical framework in which reading skills can be enhanced in the language classroom will be discussed. Specific guidelines will be examined to use for developing effective tasks that help learners improve their reading.

Chapter 7: Key Issues in the Teaching of Writing

In this chapter, a number of ways in which writing skills can be enhanced in the language classroom will be discussed. General guidelines will be provided as to how to develop effective written tasks that help learners improve their writing skills.

Chapter 8: Key Questions in Second Language Teaching: Implementing Principles of Learning

In this chapter, some of the key questions in second language teaching are formulated and possible answers will be provided.

A section on key terms is provided at the end of the book.

About the author: Alessandro Benati is Professor of Applied Linguistics and Second Language Studies at the University of Greenwich, UK. He is also Director of Research and Enterprise in the School of Humanities and Social Sciences. He has published a number of books and articles in the area of second language acquisition, foreign language grammar and language teaching methods.

Introduction

Chapter Preview

The main aim of the introduction is to present the reader with the main theoretical accounts in second language acquisition theory.

A brief overview of the main theoretical positions in language acquisition is followed by a list of possible pedagogical implications which language instructors can take into consideration in their practices.

Introduction

Second language acquisition consists of a series of hypotheses, theories and generalizations about the way learners create and develop a new language system. Second language acquisition research is a relatively new field of enquiry that has benefited from other disciplines such as linguistics, psychology and sociology and it consists of several theoretical accounts (VanPatten and Williams, 2007). One of the fundamental questions that have been addressed by scholars in this area of enquiry is how learners acquire a new linguistic system and how they can tap into that system during comprehension and speech production (VanPatten and Benati, 2010). In the last five decades, scholars have made vast progress in their understanding of how people acquire languages. Many of the advances made in understanding how people learn and develop another language system which is not their first language have provided important information for learners and language instructors. Theory and research in second language acquisition have clear implications for second language teaching practices.

These implications have been presented and discussed in many language teaching textbooks (Brown, 2001; Ellis, 1997, 2003; Larsen-Freeman, 2000; Lee and VanPatten, 1995, 2003; Nunan, 1989, 2001; Omaggio Hadley, 2001; Richards and Rodgers, 2001).

In this introductory chapter we present a brief overview of the main theoretical accounts in second language acquisition and we outline the main implications for language teaching.

Theoretical Accounts

Theories and research in second language acquisition have been developed in the attempt to understand how L2 learners come to develop their competence in a second language. Research into first language acquisition has provided good insights into the processes involved in the acquisition of a second language. Corder (1967) has suggested that, like children, L2 learners come equipped with something internal, something that guides and constrains their acquisition of the formal properties of a new language. He called this 'the internal syllabus' which develops implicitly and does not necessarily match the syllabus that instruction attempts to impose upon learners. He also made a distinction between input and intake, defining input as the language available from the environment – everything that one hears or reads in the environment, but intake as language that actually makes its way into the learner's internal system. Selinker (1972) has suggested that learners develop an internal linguistic system which he called 'interlanguage'. This system is neither the first language nor the second language, but something in-between that learners build from environmental data. A great deal of the theorizing about second language acquisition has been undertaken with language pedagogy in mind, for example White's Universal Grammar (White, 2003); Krashen's Monitor Model (Krashen, 1982); Long's Interaction Hypothesis (Long, 1996; Gass 1997); Pieneman's Processability Theory (Pieneman, 1984, 1987, 1998); VanPatten's Input Processing Theory (VanPatten, 1996, 2002, 2004); DeKeyser's Skill-learning Theory (DeKeyser, 2006).

Many of the views in second language acquisition theory, directly and/or indirectly, address some of the key issues on the role of instruction in second language teaching.

The Universal Grammar approach applies Chomsky's theory to the study of second language development (White, 2003). According to Chomsky (1975), a child possesses knowledge of language universals (Universal Grammar) and generates from that knowledge a series of hypotheses about the particular first language the child is learning. These hypotheses are modified and corrected in the light of the input to which the child is exposed. Chomsky sees first language acquisition as characterized by two main factors: an internal mechanism (language acquisition device) that is innate; and the input children are exposed to in their environment. For Chomsky, learners have their own internal syllabus to follow and the role of the teacher is reduced from that of structuring the learning path to presenting the 'linguistic data' which the student reacts to and manipulates in order to internalize a set of rules.

The pedagogical implications of this view are that language instructors should provide L2 learners with linguistic input. Some scholars believe that the acquisition of a first language is a similar process to the acquisition of a second language. Like children, adults do not need to be taught grammar in order to become fluent native speakers. This view is consistent with the Communicative Language Teaching approach (see Chapter 1).

Krashen's Monitor Model (1982) suggests that L2 learners acquire language mainly through exposure to comprehensible input, in a similar fashion to how they acquire their first language. The input that L2 learners receive should be simplified with the use of contextual and extra linguistic clues. According to the Monitor Theory, learners should be exposed to comprehensible input and they should be provided with opportunities to focus on meaning rather than grammatical forms. In Krashen's view the grammatical features of a new language are acquired by L2 learners in a specific order. When learners acquire a second language they develop two systems that are independent from each other. The 'acquisition system' (unconscious and implicit) is activated when we are engaged in communication, whereas the 'learning system' (conscious and explicit) functions as a monitor and corrector of our production. It is paramount that learners are exposed to comprehensible input and learn a second language (L2) in a very relaxed environment which enhances their motivation and does not pressurize them. This is a theory that had obvious pedagogical implications for language instructors (see Chapter 1 below) and was translated into an approach to language teaching called the Natural Approach. In a nutshell, this theory suggests that second language teaching should focus on providing learners with a rich variety of comprehensible input and opportunities to use language spontaneously and meaningfully.

The Interaction Hypothesis (Pica, 1994; Long, 1996; Gass, 1997; Gass and Mackey, 2007) focuses on how interactions might affect acquisition. In the Interaction Hypothesis input is considered a vital ingredient for the acquisition of a second language. Interactional input refers to input received during interaction where there is some kind of communicative exchange involving the learner and at least one other person (e.g. conversation, classroom interactions). Through these interactions, learners have the advantage of being able to negotiate meaning and make some conversational adjustments. This means that conversation and interaction make linguistics features salient to the learner who may be able to notice specific linguistic features they would not notice otherwise. The ability for language learners to notice might have an effect on their acquisition of a new language. How learners are led to notice things can happen in several ways. Learners can be exposed to modified input. Input modifications happen when the other speaker adjusts his or her speech due to perceived difficulties in learner comprehension. Learners can receive some corrective feedback. The other speaker indicates in some way that the learner has produced something non-native-like. Conversational interaction and negotiation can also facilitate acquisition. Learners sometimes request clarifications or repetitions if they do not understand the input they receive. In the attempt to facilitate acquisition, one person can request the other to modify his/her utterances or the person modifies its own utterances to be understood. Among the techniques used for modifying interaction the most common are: (1) clarification request (e.g. what did you say?); (2) confirmation checks (e.g. did you say....); (3) comprehension checks (e.g. do you understand?).

For the Interaction Hypothesis, comprehensible input might not be sufficient to develop native-like grammatical competence and L2 learners also need comprehensible output (Swain, 1985, 1995).

Learners need 'pushed output' that is speech or writing that will force learners to produce language correctly, precisely and appropriately. According to Swain (1995: 249), 'producing the language might be the trigger that forces the learner to pay attention to the means of expression needed in order to successfully convey his or her own intended meaning'. Input, interaction, feedback and output are the main components of the Interaction Hypothesis. This theory has a series of pedagogical implications for second language teaching. Language instructors should give L2 learners the opportunities to communicate and interact with each other at all times during instruction. Learners should be involved in learning tasks where they have opportunities to communicate and negotiate meaning. Enhancing the input through the use of different techniques (see Chapter 2 in this book) might be sufficient in helping learners pay attention to the formal properties of a targeted language without the need for metalinguistic discussion.

The Processability Theory (Pieneman, 1984, 1987, 1998) is based on research which focuses on interlanguage developments. This theory advanced by Pienemann (1984, 1987, 1998) aims at investigating whether formal instruction would alter acquisitional sequences. Research findings show that instruction does not promote the acquisition of any developmental features out of sequence. In Pienemann's view, instruction can promote language acquisition if the interlanguage is close to the point when the structure to be taught is acquired in the natural setting. The teachability hypothesis relies on the possibility that instruction could help the learner to alter the natural route of development, if the learner is psycholinguistically ready. Therefore, according to Pienemann, instruction can facilitate the second language acquisition process if it coincides with the moment when the learner is ready.

Learners follow a very rigid route in the acquisition of grammatical structures. Structures become learnable only when the previous steps on this acquisitional path have been reached. Pienemann's conclusions could be summarized as follows: stages of acquisition cannot be skipped; instruction will be beneficial if it focuses on structures tailored to the next developmental stage. In his Processability Theory Pienemann (1998) argues that internal psycholinguistics factors and processing constraints determine the sequences of acquisition of features in a targeted language. Pienemann's processing procedures are acquired in the following progressive sequence: word—category—phrase—sentence. Once learners have recognized the meaning of a word they can assign words to a lexical category and function. If it is true that learners pass through predictable stages while acquiring the grammatical system of a second language, the pedagogical implications of this theory are that language instructors must choose the right moment to provide language instruction. It is not a matter of whether or not instruction has a role to play but a matter of timing. Instructors must take into consideration that learners will not be able to produce forms or structures for which they are not psycholinguistically ready.

The Input Processing Theory (VanPatten, 1996, 2002, 2004) refers to how learners perceive and detect formal features of language input, and the strategies or mechanisms that guide and direct how L2 learners do this. According to Van Patten only a small portion of the input that L2 learners are exposed to is processed and becomes intake. This is due to learners' processing limitations and processing problems in decoding the input. Learners seem to process input for meaning (words) before they process for form (grammatical features).

In a sentence such as 'Yesterday I watched my son playing in the park' which contains a lexical feature encoding a particular meaning (temporal reference 'yesterday'), learners will tend to process the lexical item (Yesterday) before the grammatical form (-*ed*) as both encode the same meaning. This processing strategy called 'Lexical Preference Strategy' causes learners to skip grammatical features in the input. Another processing problem examined by the input processing theory is when L2 learners parse sentences as they need to figure out who did what to whom. Normally, they parse sentences relying on word order and employ a first noun processing strategy that assigns subject or agent status to the first noun or pronoun they encounter in a sentence. In the sentence 'Paul was kissed by Mary', learners assign the role of agent to the first noun or noun phrase in the sentence and therefore misinterpret the sentence as it was Paul who kissed Mary. In some cases this can cause delay in learning as learners might misinterpret the input they receive (e.g. languages have different syntactic structures with different word orders). Research on input processing has attempted to describe the linguistic data learners attend to during comprehension and what data they do not attend to, for example what grammatical roles learners assign to nouns or how the position in an utterance influences what gets processed. These processing principles seem to provide an explanation of what learners are doing with input when they are asked to comprehend it. Manipulating the input might help learners to process grammar more efficiently and accurately. Changing the way L2 learners process input and enriching their intake might have an effect on the developing system that subsequently should have an impact on how learners produce the target language. VanPatten's input theory has important pedagogical implications for second language teaching. Grammar instruction should be aimed at changing the way input is perceived and processed by L2 language learners. Learners should be exposed to meaningful input that contains many instances of the same grammatical meaning-form relationship (e.g. verb ending *-ed* encodes a past event). Grammar instruction should guide and focus learners' attention when they process input.

Skill-learning Theory (DeKeyser, 2006) is related to a cognitive and information processing model. According to this model, second language acquisition is generated from exposure to input and the ability of L2 learners to process information and to build a network of associations. Second language acquisition entails going from controlled mode of operation (declarative knowledge) to automatic mode (procedural knowledge) through repeated practice. This theory addresses issues related to the way people develop fluency and accuracy. Accuracy refers to the ability to do something correctly while fluency refers to the speed with which a person can do something. Theoretically, the features of accuracy and fluency can develop independently of each other so that someone could be highly accurate but exceedingly slow at doing something, or exceedingly fast but highly inaccurate. In reality, research on skill development has shown that the two tend to develop in tandem. As accuracy increases, so does speed. The theory has pedagogical implications for second language teaching.

The learner is the central figure in the acquisition process, and needs to practice until patterns are well established (fluency). Input, interaction and feedback can speed up second language acquisition.

Many scholars (VanPatten, 2003; Williams, 2005) have attempted to highlight some of the basic principles in second language acquisition:

- There are two types of language knowledge (explicit and implicit).
- Acquisition and skill acquisition are two separate processes.
- Input is a necessary ingredient for acquisition.
- Attention is a key element in acquisition.
- Acquisition takes a long time but it is a dynamic process.

The reader ought to consider these short theoretical account descriptions and principles here as 'advanced organizers' for reading more detailed and sometimes more technical material on second language acquisition theory and research (see suggested reading section below). Despite the fact that research and theory in second language learning do not provide a uniform account of how learning happens and particularly how instruction can best facilitate language acquisition, clear progress has been made in gaining a better understanding of the processes involved in acquiring another language and developing effective classroom teaching. A set of generalizations for second language teaching might be drawn from theory and research in second language acquisition.

These generalizations might serve as the basis for offering practical suggestions for language teaching.

Pedagogic Implications

Theory and research in second language acquisition emphasize the complexity of acquisition processes. They have provided the following insights into language acquisition that might be useful in developing an effective language teaching approach:

1. Internal and implicit processes responsible for language acquisition are similar regardless of learners' first language. Learners process grammar often following a natural order and a specific sequence (i.e. they master different grammatical structures in a relatively fixed and universal order and they pass through a sequence of stages of learning on route to mastering each grammatical structure).
2. Learners require extensive second language input exposure to build their internal new linguistic systems. Input needs to be easily comprehensible and message oriented in order to be processed effectively by learners. Research has shown that learners focus primarily on meaning when they process elements of the new language.
3. Interaction with other speakers is a key factor to promote acquisition.

4. Acquisition requires learners to make form-function connections – the relation between a particular form and its meaning(s).
5. In the view of most researchers, acquisition of a second language is primarily a matter of developing implicit knowledge.
6. Language acquisition requires opportunities for output practice. Language production serves to generate better input through the feedback that learners' efforts at production elicit.

Language instructors should aim at developing a principled evidence-based approach to language teaching based on our knowledge about language acquisition theory and research. This 'approach' should have the following characteristics:

a) Instruction needs to be predominantly directed at developing implicit knowledge taking into consideration orders and stages of development in learners.
b) Instruction needs to provide learners with comprehensible, simplified, modified and message-oriented input. Instruction should focus on providing opportunities for the learners to use language spontaneously and meaningfully. Corrective feedback in the form of recasting could provide more opportunities for input exposure.
c) Instruction needs to create opportunities for interaction and negotiation of meaning among speakers. Interaction fosters learning when a communication problem arises and learners are engaged in resolving it through interaction and negotiation of meaning.
d) Instruction needs to provide opportunities to focus on grammatical form within a communicative context. Grammar approaches that promote learning are: input flood, textual enhancement, consciousness raising and structured input practice (see Key Terms section).
e) Instruction must provide learners with an opportunity to participate in communicative tasks to develop implicit knowledge. Learners need to be involved in communicative tasks (using a variety of discourse type activities such as role-plays and storytelling) which require them to take responsibilities in communication.
f) Instruction must create opportunities for learners to communicate by performing communicative functions (output). Whenever learners produce language it should be for the purpose of expressing some kind of meaning. Meaning should be emphasized over form.

Suggested Reading

Gass, S., and Selinker, L. (2008). *Second Language Acquisition: An Introductory Course.* New York: Routledge.

This is an introductory book on second language acquisition which takes a multidisciplinary perspective in presenting theory and research in this field of enquiry.

Ortega, L. (2008). *Understanding Second Language Acquisition.* Oxford: Oxford University Press.

This book offers an excellent introduction to theories and research paradigms in the field of second language acquisition.

VanPatten, B. (2003). *From Input to Output: A Teacher's Guide to Second Language Acquisition.* New York: McGraw-Hill.

This volume provides an overview of key issues in second language acquisition research. The author gives a compelling account of current research and theory while providing opportunity for discussion and reflection on issues of particular relevance to classroom practitioners.

VanPatten, B., and Williams, J. (eds) (2007). *Theories in Second Language Acquisition.* Mahwah, NJ: Erlbaum.

This is an introductory book and survey on the main theoretical accounts of second language acquisition. Each chapter presents a single theory and analyses the claims and evidence supporting the theory.

VanPatten, B., and Benati, A. (2010). *Key Terms in Second Language Acquisition.* London: Continuum.

This book defines and explains key terms in second language acquisition. It also addresses and explains the key issues in second language acquisition research.

1 Key Developments in Second Language Teaching

Chapter Preview

In this chapter a brief review of some of the key teaching methodologies/approaches in second language teaching is provided, from the Grammar Translation Method, to the Communicative Language Teaching and Task-based Instruction approach.

Guidelines for adopting a principled evidence-based approach to second language teaching will be offered at the end of this chapter.

Introduction

Language instructors are always interested in finding out what is the most effective and efficient way to teach languages. They often look at innovative techniques in teaching grammar, correcting errors and engaging L2 learners in appropriate and effective language tasks. In the last fifty years we have witnessed a variety of methods and approaches in second language teaching (e.g. the Grammar Translation Method, the Direct Method, the Audio-lingual Method, Total Physical Response, the Natural Approach, Communicative Language Teaching, Content-based Instruction, and Task-based Instruction). Despite the fact that most of these methods have been developed on the basis of a particular theoretical view on the way language is learned, it is now understood that language instructors should not look at 'the right method' to teach languages.

Language instructors should instead be aware of the advances made in second language acquisition theories, the main findings of empirical research, and new insights into the ways languages are learned, in order to utilize a principled evidence-based approach to second language teaching. This 'new approach', based on principles/theories and evidence from second language acquisition research and other relevant disciplines (e.g.

psycholinguistics, psychology) would inform language instructors on what is the most effective and efficient way to approach the teaching of grammar, the correction of errors and the development of effective language tasks.

Since the 1970s scholars and practitioners have proposed alternative approaches to second language teaching. This was in response to traditional methods of organizing language teaching which consisted essentially of presenting and explaining grammatical features of a target language and engaging L2 learners in output-based practice. In this chapter, we provide a brief overview of the emergence of different methods and approaches to second language teaching.

Key Developments

The 1950s and Before

The Grammar Translation Method was originally used in the teaching of Latin and Greek. It was used to help L2 learners to study foreign language literature. It was the main teaching method used in many European countries between the 1840s and the 1940s. One of the main tenets of this method is that learners need to develop the ability to read a text in another language and to translate the text from one language into another. The main principles of the Grammar Translation Method were:

- the role of the teacher is very authoritative and the learner's native language is the medium for instruction. It is a very teacher-centred method of teaching;
- learning consists of being able to read and translate a text into and out of the target language;
- the focus of teaching is to develop the learner's ability to read, to write and to translate;
- the grammar is taught systematically (following a sequencing grammar syllabus) through explicit teaching of grammatical rules. The main assumption is that a second language is learned through the deduction of the grammatical properties of a target L2. This would then allow learners to develop a conscious and explicit representation of that language;
- errors are corrected;
- learners should memorize vocabulary items;
- the main goal for instruction is the ability to attain high proficiency

standards in translation and accuracy. The ability to communicate using the target language is not the main goal for instruction.

Based on these principles, a variety of techniques were developed to help learners translate, practise and memorize the new language (see Table 1.1).

Table 1.1 Grammar Translation Method techniques

– Read and translate a literary passage
– Reading and comprehension activities
– Deductive grammar practice
– Fill-in-the-blanks
– Memorization practice
– Composition

The Direct Method was proposed as a result of the failure of the Grammar Translation Method to encourage L2 learners to use the target language to communicate. According to this method, language instructors should provide learners with opportunities to convey meaning through use of the new language. The Direct Method differs from the Grammar Translation Method in the way the teaching of grammar is approached. Instructors should approach the teaching of grammar inductively. This is on the assumption that L2 learners should learn grammar by interpreting contextual and situational cues rather than receiving long explanations. Learners should be continuously exposed to the target language and teachers should not use the learner's native language.

The main principles of the Direct Method were:

- language instructors, teachers and learners are more like partners. Learners are given opportunities to interact with other learners. In this sense, this method is less teacher-centred. The target language should always be used in the classroom;
- learners are encouraged to make links between meaning and the language. The emphasis is on spoken language and vocabulary is emphasized over grammar;
- grammar is taught inductively. Learners need to discover the rules of grammar;
- errors are not corrected as teachers should provide opportunities for self-correction;
- learning of words is emphasized over grammar. Developing the ability to communicate orally is emphasized.

Some of the typical activities of this method to language teaching are summarized in Table 1.2.

Table 1.2 Direct Method activities

– Read texts aloud
– Question and answer tasks
– Fill-in-the-blanks
– Conversation tasks
– Dictation
– Self-correction

The 1960s

In the late 1950s and the beginning of the 1960s, a new method in second language teaching, called the Audio-lingual Method, was developed. This method was underpinned by a second language learning theory called *Behaviourism*. The behaviourist's view is in strong opposition to Chomsky's view (1965) who assumes that humans have innate language knowledge and that they are genetically programmed to develop our linguistic system in certain ways. Behaviourism maintained that it is the learners' experience which is largely responsible for language learning and it is more important than any innate capacity. The behaviourist theory (Skinner, 1957) argued that the child's mind is a *tabula rasa* and good language habits are learned through the process of repetition, imitation and reinforcement. According to theorists, language learning is a progressive accumulation of habits and the ultimate goal is to produce language which is error-free. The first language was seen as a major obstacle to the acquisition of a second language since it caused interference errors (caused by habits in the L1) and negative transfer (from L1 to L2) of habits. It was believed that language learning proceeded from form to meaning, i.e. first master the grammatical forms and then move to express meaning. Supporters of this theory saw language learning as a process of acquiring verbal habits. The main conditions for acquiring these habits were:

1. the learner imitated the language heard;
2. the imitation has to be rewarded;
3. as a result of this, the behaviour is repeated and becomes habitual.

This theory was translated into the Audio-lingual Method which empha-sized the use of memorization and mechanical and pattern drills practice. The main principles of the Audio-lingual Method were:

- language instructors play the role of leaders and are responsible for providing a good language model. Learners must imitate this model by following instructions and practices. Learners are always exposed to the target language;
- learners are exposed to correct models/patterns of the target L2. Practice consists of a type of exercise called 'drills practice' (e.g. repetition and substitution/transformation drills). L2 learners have to repeat, manipulate or transform a particular form or structure in order to complete a task;
- learners follow a very structural syllabus;
- learners engage in activities which focus on structure and form rather than meaning and are corrected for inaccurate imitations;
- learners must become accurate in the target L2. Linguistic compe-tence is the main goal of instruction.

The main activities which dominated a classroom lesson in the Audio-lin-gual Method are provided in Table 1.3.

Table 1.3 Audio-lingual Method activities

• Dialogue memorization
• Patter drills:
– Repetition drills
– Transformation drills
– Chain drills
– Question-and-answer drills

The 1970s and 1980s

The 1970s and 1980s are two periods in which a number of innovative meth-ods/approaches emerged (e.g. Total Physical Response, Natural Approach and Communicative Language Teaching).

James Asher's Total Physical Response (1977) is a comprehension-based approach to language teaching. It is based on the assumption that language learning should start with understanding the language we hear or read before we proceed to production. A set of principles were set to help L2 learners to increase their understanding:

- instructors provide L2 learners with a nonverbal model that they need to imitate. Only after an initial period of comprehension of the target language, learners will be able to speak;
- initially, language instructors issue commands and then perform the actions with students. Later on, students demonstrate an understanding of the commands by performing them alone;
- vocabulary and grammar learning are the skills emphasized. Understanding should precede producing. When ready to speak, teachers should let students make errors and should be tolerant.

The main activities used in Total Physical Response are summarized in Table 1.4.

Table 1.4 Total Physical Response activities

- Using commands to direct behaviour
- Role reversal
- Action sequence

Another comprehension-based approach to second language teaching is the so-called Natural Approach (Krashen and Terrell, 1983). This approach is based on the Monitor Model Theory developed by Krashen (1982) in the late 1970s. According to Krashen, there is a need for the creation of a kind of environment in the L2 classroom that resembles the condition where L1 learning takes place. He hypothesized that if L2 learners were exposed to 'comprehensible' input and were provided with opportunities to focus on meaning and messages rather than grammatical forms and accuracy, they would be able to acquire the L2 in much the same way as L1 learners. Krashen's Monitor Model Theory is based on five hypotheses:

1. In the Acquisition–Learning Distinction, Krashen (1982) claims that learners have both an 'acquired' system and a 'learned' system which are totally separate. The 'learned' system is the result of the process of paying attention to the language in order to understand the rules. L2 learning is the conscious construction of rules in the pedagogical context. The 'acquired' system is, according to Krashen, a subconscious and intuitive process which arises when learners are

involved in using language in actual communication and is similar to the child's construction of an L1 language system. It seems that, for Krashen, L2 acquisition and learning are two autonomous processes. According to him, explicit knowledge cannot be converted into implicit knowledge – they are completely separate.

2. In the Natural Order Hypothesis, Krashen maintains that acquisition of grammatical structures (morphemes) proceeds in a predictable order when that acquisition is natural (not via formal learning). Krashen accepts that formal instruction contributes to the learning of explicit knowledge, although he sees this as a limited role. The role of explicit learning of rules in classroom instruction is to monitor output; there is no conversion into acquired and automatic language ability (Monitor Hypothesis).

3. According to Krashen, the system we learn consciously plays a subordinate role and enables us to monitor what we produce and increase its accuracy.

4. Instruction should focus on providing a rich variety of comprehensible input and opportunities for the learners to use language in spontaneous and meaningful interaction (Input Hypothesis). Only comprehensible input is effective in increasing proficiency, whereas correction, output and more teaching of grammar do not, according to the Input Hypothesis.

5. The Affective Filter Hypothesis controls how much input the learner has received and how much it was converted into intake. Learners' characteristics such as high motivation, low anxiety and high self-confidence are effective variables promoting success in second language acquisition (SLA). If this is the case, a learner will obtain more input for L2 acquisition through interaction when their filter is low.

There are certain practical implications for classroom practice consistent with Krashen's theory which forms the basis of Terrell's Natural Approach (Krashen and Terrell, 1983).

The main principles of this approach are:

*   language instructors should provide good, comprehensible and message-oriented input for acquisition. They should create a good classroom atmosphere in which there is low filter for learning (i.e. learners are not under pressure to produce the target language), and orchestrate a wide range of classroom activities. Error correction has a negative effect on motivation and attitude and it causes embarrassment;

- language instruction should focus on communicative competence rather than on grammatical perfection. The main function of language teaching is to provide comprehensible input;
- language instruction has to aim at the modification and improvement of the student's developing grammar rather than at building up that grammar. Most, if not all, classroom activities should be designed to evoke communication and not wasted in grammatical lectures or manipulative exercises;
- teachers should create the opportunity for students to acquire rather than force them to learn language. Affective rather than cognitive factors are primary in language learning;
- the key to comprehension and oral production is the acquisition of vocabulary.

These types of activities (comprehension activities, commands which involve the use of single words or short phrases, role-plays and group problem-solving) dominate the classroom lesson in the Natural Approach (see Table 1.5).

Table 1.5 Natural Approach activities

- Comprehension (pre-production) activities which are a listening comprehension practice, with no requirements for the students to speak in the target language. This consists of comprehension activities with the help of gestures and visual aids.

- Early speech production is introduced when the students have a recognition vocabulary of 500 words. Production activities require Question/Answer on the basis of a single word answer, or a sentence-completion response in which a personalized question is asked and the answer is provided except for one word, which the student supplies.

- Speech emergence occurs after the early speech production phase, and is characterized by activities such as games and problem-solving activities.

A key development in second language teaching was the emergence of the Communicative Language Teaching approach. The main assumption behind this approach is that Communicative Language Teaching programmes will lead to the development of both linguistic competence (knowledge of the rules of grammar) and communicative competence (knowledge of the rules of language use). The development of a new communicative approach to language teaching is a complex one which is related to a number of disciplines. Chomsky's criticism of behaviourist learning theories, in undermining the credibility of the Audio-lingual Method, sets the framework for a more child-centred approach which favours a highly inductive approach.

In the 1980s one could talk of a 'fever' for the Communicative Language Teaching approach. Communicative Language Teaching was considered to be a type of instruction, an approach to language teaching rather than a method. It was the growing discontent on the part of language teachers with the previous methods, together with the need for a new method, that led methodologists to find a way which would essentially bring the learner into closer contact with the target language community. Littlewood (1981) claimed that Communicative Language Teaching makes us consider language not only in terms of its structures but also in terms of the communicative functions that it performs. Therefore this approach aims at understanding what people do with language forms when they communicate. Communicative Language Teaching is a student-centred type of instruction, a revolutionary approach to foreign language teaching as it involves both teaching and learning. If the class can become 'an area of co-operative negotiation, joint interpretation, and the sharing of expression' as indicated by Breen and Candlin (1980: 14), then the teacher is in a position to give students the opportunity for spontaneous, unpredictable, exploratory production of language when involved in classroom activities. The main contribution of this new type of instruction is the shift from attention to the grammatical forms to the communicative properties of the language. The language instructor creates the opportunity and the conditions in the classroom in a communicative way. This is to say the learner has someone to talk to, something to talk about, and a desire to understand and to make himself understood. If that happens, the learning can take place naturally and teaching can be effective.

Although there are different interpretations and theoretical positions of Communicative Language Teaching, there are some general principles shared by professionals. These are:

- encourage the development of communicative competence (e.g. grammatical competence, pragmatic competence, sociolinguistic competence and strategic competence);
- take into account learners' needs;
- syllabus-based on notional–functional principles;
- a commitment to message-orientated use of the target language in the classroom.

The main characteristics of this approach are as follows.

- Meaning is emphasized over form. Genuine questions (ask questions to which students do not know the answer) as opposed to display questions (type of questions asked to make students display knowledge) are used because there is a focus on meaning rather than form.
- Learners should have considerable exposure to the second language speech from the teacher, and other learners and instructors should provide opportunities for learners to play an active role. The role of the language instructor is to construct dynamic classroom tasks (architect) and encourage the learner's participation and contribution (resource person or co-builder). To that end, the materials that the instructor uses must permit these new roles. Therefore the traditional question/answer task should be supplanted by a task-oriented activity. By providing a series of tasks to complete the tutor plays the role of architect encouraging learners to take responsibility for generating the information themselves rather than just receiving it.
- Communication is defined as the expression, interpretation and negotiation of meaning. Learners and teachers must make some mutual efforts to understand interactions and negotiate meaning. Negotiation of meaning can be defined as any interactions in which learners and their interlocutors adjust their speech phonologically, lexically and morphosyntactically to resolve difficulties in mutual understanding that impede the course of their communication.
- Comprehensible and meaning-bearing input promotes acquisition. Simplification of the input through the use of contextual props, cues and gestures also promote acquisition. Comprehension activities should be used without initial requirement for students to speak in the target language. The main function of language teaching is to provide comprehensible input (useful especially for beginners and foreign language learners) which leads to a low filter (high motivation and low anxiety). Little pressure should be exercised for learners to perform at a high level of accuracy and, in the early stages, comprehension is emphasized over production.
- Classroom activities should be designed to evoke communication and not be wasted in grammatical lectures or manipulative and mechanical exercises.
- Learners must be involved in learning tasks which allow them to perform a range of communicative functions with the target L2. Communicative Language Teaching should encourage the use of a variety of discourse tasks (e.g. role-playing).

- Grammar should be learned communicatively. Learners should be provided with communicative tasks that contain enough samples of the linguistic features that learners are trying to learn. Learners must be engaged in communicative tasks where grammar is enhanced using different techniques (e.g. input enhancement, consciousness raising, processing instruction).
- The amount of correction in the L2 classroom must be kept to a minimum, as the emphasis must be to allow learners to express themselves. In Communicative Language Teaching, error correction is seen as having a negative effect on learners in terms of lowering their motivation and affecting their attitude. An alternative form of correction might be done by the teacher by repeating what the students have said with the correct form (recasting) or using other forms of corrective feedback such as negative enhancement techniques. Negative enhancement techniques would involve providing learners with some information about the incorrectness of the particular use of a form/structure by enhancing the mistake in different ways (e.g. a facial expression or offering a quizzical look).

The main activities used in Communicative Language Teaching are summarized in Table 1.6.

Table 1.6 Communicative Language Teaching activities

- Role-plays
- Language games
- Scrambled sentences
- Communicative grammar tasks
- Exchange information tasks
- Discourse type tasks
- Picture story

The 1990s and 2000s

A similar approach to the Communicative Language Teaching approach is the so-called Content-based Instruction approach. Two of the key features of this approach are: communication is central to the teaching; and learners are encouraged to use the target language to learn it (Met, 1999).

According to this approach, language instructors should integrate the learning of a target language (e.g. English, Spanish) with another content or subject matter (e.g. Geography, History). Crandall and Tucker (1990: 83) define the integrative component of Content-based Instruction as 'drawing topics, texts, and tasks from content or subject-matter classes, but focusing on the cognitive, academic, language skills required to participate effectively in content instruction'.

The main characteristics of this approach are:

- subject matter content is used for teaching purposes and language instructors need to provide learners with assistance in understanding subject matter texts;
- learners are highly motivated and are exposed to authentic material and tasks;
- language is used to convey specific content.

Immersion programmes, which use a Content-based Instruction approach, are considered very successful programmes with respect to the proficiency levels attained by L2 learners. However, immersion learners do not attain native-like proficiency in speaking and writing. It is believed that one of the reasons for this is due to instructional matters. Most immersion language instructors focus their attention on the instruction of subject matter content. The lack of a systematic approach to the teaching of specific form or language structures in meaningful contexts and the lack of corrective feedback contribute to less than optimal levels of proficiency in immersion students (Lyster and Ranta, 1997).

Classroom-based research conducted in the 1980s and 90s has suggested that focusing on the grammatical properties of a target language is a necessary ingredient in second language development. This research emphasized the need for a 'focus on form' (Ellis, 1991; Doughty and Williams, 1998; Spada, 1997) in second language teaching; the need for output practice (Swain, 1995); the need to enhance the quality of the input received by L2 learners in the classroom (Sharwood-Smith, 1991, 1993); and the quality of input processing (VanPatten, 1996). In the 1980s and the 1990s second language learning scholars and researchers also suggested that psycholinguistics factors and processing conditions are relevant for second language acquisition. It was believed that instruction in which L2 learners are given communicative real-world tasks to complete in which they have opportunities for exposure to comprehensible and meaningful input, opportunities for interaction and negotiation of meaning, might ultimately engage natural acquisitional mechanisms, cause a change in L2 learners' interlanguage system and drive forward development.

Task-based Instruction was developed in the late 1980s (see Nunan, 1989) and became popular in the 1990s. It referred to a type of language teaching which takes 'tasks' as its key units for designing and implementing language instruction. Task-based Instruction should enhance language acquisition by:

- providing learners with opportunities to make the language input they receive more comprehensible;
- furnishing contexts in which learners need to produce output which others can understand;
- making the classroom closer to real-life language situations.

Task-based Instruction aims at providing L2 learners with a natural context to use the target language. Learners work to complete a task and have plenty of opportunities for interaction and negotiation of meaning as they have to understand each other and express their own meaning. The essential characteristics of a task in this approach are:

- meaning must play a key role;
- learners must resolve a real-world communication problem;
- learners will be assessed in terms of the task outcome.

Task-based Instruction aims at integrating all four language skills and providing opportunities for the learners to experiment with and explore both spoken and written language through learning activities which are designed to engage learners in the authentic, practical and functional use of language for meaningful purposes (i.e. to cultivate the learners' communicative competence).

A traditional model for the organization of language lessons, both in the classroom and in course-books, has long been the PPP approach (presentation, practice, production). With this model individual language items are presented by the teacher, then practised in the form of spoken and written exercises (often pattern drills), and then used by the learners in less controlled speaking or writing activities.

Another model is the Test-Teach-Test approach (TTT), in which the production stage comes first and the learners are 'thrown in at the deep end' and required to perform a particular task (a role-play, for example). This is followed by the teacher dealing with some of the grammatical or lexical problems that arose in the first stage and the learners then being required either to perform the initial task again or to perform a similar task.

Task-based Instruction is an alternative model which is based on sound theoretical foundations and one which takes account of the need for authentic communication. The roles assumed by L2 learners and teachers during Task-based Instruction are very similar to the general roles taken by learners and language instructors in Communicative Language Teaching and will be also influenced by the specific tasks used. The procedure used in Task-based Instruction is as follows:

- *Pre-task activities*: L2 learners are involved in pre-task activities such as brainstorming and problem-solving tasks to introduce the topic and the situation of a given task.
- *Task activity*: L2 learners work in pairs or groups with a task and all the different steps and cues provided to complete the task.
- *Post-task activities*: L2 learners are given opportunities to compare how they perform in the task.

The activities used in Task-based Instruction are summarized in Table 1.7.

Table 1.7 Task-based Instruction activities

- Jigsaw tasks, which involve L2 learners combining different pieces of information.
- Information-gap tasks, which involve L2 learners finding out a set of information to complete the task.
- Problem-solving tasks, which involve L2 learners finding a solution to 'a problem'.
- Decision making tasks, which involve L2 learners identifying a problem and possible outcomes.
- Opinion exchange tasks, which involve L2 learners engaging in discussion and exchange ideas.

Key Implications

Language instructors are always interested in finding out the best way to teach languages. In the last fifty years we have witnessed a variety of methods in language teaching (e.g. Grammar Translation, Natural Approach,

Total Physical Response, Audio-lingual Method, Communicative Language Teaching, and Task-based Instruction). However, instructors should not look for 'the right method' to teach languages, as there is not a particular method that is more effective than another. Instead, language instructors should be interested in finding out the best way to address practical issues in second language teaching: teaching grammar, correcting errors, and so on.

In order to provide teachers with answers to practical questions in second language teaching, we should look at solutions, suggestions and principles that are grounded in theory and empirical evidence. An 'approach' for language teaching should draw from theories and research on instructed second language acquisition. Language instructors can combine elements as long as their choices are guided and informed by theory and empirical research in language learning and teaching. Therefore a new approach to language teaching must be informed by specific principles derived from theory and must be evidence-based (based on findings from empirical research in instructed second language acquisition).

A key principle in second language teaching is that communication is at the heart of language acquisition. L2 learners acquire a language by engaging in the interpretation, expression and negotiation of meaning. Based on theory and research in instructed second language acquisition, some overall guidelines for teachers, for an 'effective approach' to language teaching, are provided below:

1. Teachers should plan language tasks so that L2 learners actively participate and contribute to their learning through the completion of a communicative task.
2. Teachers should prepare L2 learners for the interpretation, expression and negotiation of meaning in speaking, reading and writing activities.
3. Teachers should make sure that, in language tasks, meaning is emphasized over form.
4. Teacher should make sure that L2 learners are exposed to comprehensible and simplified input to increase the amount and quality of the input that learners intake.
5. Teachers should use a variety of discourse type activities such as role-playing, communicative tasks, stories, real-life materials.
6. Teachers should approach grammar teaching through the use of a variety of input enhancement techniques.
7. Teacher should make sure that the amount of correction is kept to a minimum, letting L2 learners express themselves.

8. Teachers should design group work tasks, where L2 learners are encouraged to negotiate meaning, use a variety of linguistic forms and functions and develop overall fluency skills. Teachers should provide learner-centred instruction as supposed to teacher-learned instruction.

In the next chapters we will address some of the key issues in second language teaching with the intention of providing some effective suggestions and solutions for second language teachers.

Suggested Reading

Hinkel, E. (2005) (ed.). *Handbook of Research in Second Language Teaching and Learning*. Mahwah, NJ: Lawrence Erlbaum Associates.

This handbook is a useful guide as it provides an up-to-date overview of current knowledge and research into second language teaching.

Larsen-Freeman, D. (2000). *Techniques and Principles in Language Teaching*. Oxford: Oxford University Press.

This volume provides a good introduction to language teaching methodologies from the Grammar Translation Method to current teaching methods. The book is an extremely good resource for teachers as it offers a step-by-step guide to different approaches and techniques of language teaching.

Lee, J., and VanPatten, B. (2003). *Making Communicative Language Teaching Happen*. New York: McGraw-Hill.

The focus of this volume is on a particular approach to language teaching called the Communicative Language Teaching approach. It provides readers with a comprehensive analysis of what this is, why it can be justified and how it can be implemented.

Long, M. H., and Doughty, C. J. (eds) (2009). *The Handbook of Language Teaching*. Oxford: Wiley-Blackwell.

This handbook is an invaluable resource for language teachers and students. It provides the reader with an overall view on research and practices in second and foreign language teaching.

Richards, J. C., and Rodgers, T. S. (2001). *Approaches and Methods in Language Teaching*. Cambridge: Cambridge University Press.

This volume gives an accurate account of various approaches and methods in second language teaching. It provides readers with an examination of the different characteristics of each method and/or approach emphasizing strengths and weaknesses.

VanPatten, B. (2003). *From Input to Output: A Teacher's Guide to Second Language Acquisition*. New York: McGraw-Hill.

This volume provides teachers with an accessible overview of key issues in second language acquisition research. It provides a comprehensive discussion on topics related to second language learning that are relevant to second language teaching.

2 Key Issues in Grammar Teaching

Chapter Preview

In this chapter, several approaches/techniques to grammar instruction will be examined. An analysis of input-based options to grammar instruction will be provided (e.g. processing instruction practice; input enhancement techniques).

A review of one popular structured-based option to grammar instruction, namely consciousness raising, will be presented. Finally, output-based options to grammar instruction such as collaborative output tasks will be examined.

The chapter concludes with a reflection on research and practices on the teaching of grammar and provides some overall guidelines and suggestions for language instructors.

Introduction

One of the key issues in second language teaching concerns the role and practice of grammar instruction. Does grammar instruction make a difference? How do we teach grammar in the language classroom? Is there an effective technique to teach grammar that is better than others? These are some of the questions that scholars, language instructors and practitioners address in their attempt to find the most appropriate and effective way to teach grammar. While many scholars address some of these questions to develop a better understanding of how people learn grammar, language instructors are in search of the most effective way to approach the teaching of grammar in the language classroom. In this chapter we examine the way the role and the practice of grammar teaching have changed over the years. As outlined by Nassaji and Fotos (2011: 1), these changes 'have been due to a number of theoretical and empirical developments in the field'. The main theoretical and pedagogical views around the role of grammar instruction will be presented in this chapter.

More specifically, this chapter will provide a brief examination of a variety of approaches to grammar teaching and offer a list of principles and guidelines that teachers should consider to design and implement effective grammar tasks during their teaching. One of the key issues in grammar teaching highlighted by Lee and VanPatten (2003) is not whether or not we should teach grammar but how we incorporate a teaching grammar component in our communicative language teaching practices.

Key Aspects

In this chapter, input-based and output-based options to grammar teaching will be examined (interactional approaches to grammar instruction will be discussed in the following chapter). The main key terms used in this chapter are:

- Processing instruction practice
- Input enhancement techniques
- Consciousness raising tasks
- Collaborative output tasks.

Processing instruction refers to a psycholinguistics approach to grammar teaching which aims at pushing learners away from incorrect processing strategies towards more appropriate ones. The main role of this approach is to enable L2 learners to make efficient form-meaning connections in the input.

Input enhancement techniques refer to different manipulations of aural or written input to make grammatical elements of a target language more salient in the input. The main role of these techniques is to enable L2 learners to notice forms/structures in the input that might otherwise go unnoticed.

Consciousness raising tasks refer to a structured grammar teaching technique in which L2 learners are asked to solve a grammatical problem. The main role of these tasks is to enable L2 learners to develop their conscious representation of the target grammatical form/structure.

Collaborative output tasks refer to a variety of output-based grammar techniques that elicit output but also promote focus on form (e.g. dictogloss, reconstruction cloze tasks, jigsaw tasks, structured output tasks).

Key Developments

Does instruction make a difference? In the early eighties, this was a key question in instructed second language acquisition research. It was raised by Michael Long (1983) who presented the results of a number of empirical studies addressing the main question as to whether instruction can be beneficial for second language learners. His review was partly inconclusive but it provided the stimulus for other researchers to address the same question through empirical and classroom-based research. Since 1983, scholars have investigated and examined the role of grammar instruction and more specifically the effectiveness of different techniques to teach grammar in the language classroom. Techniques proposed to teach grammar have often been related to emerging theoretical views in second language acquisition.

In the field of instructed second language acquisition research, there are two main theoretical views on the role of instruction (see VanPatten and Benati, 2010 for a review on the role of instruction): the first position is that instruction is limited and constrained; the second position asserts that instruction is beneficial.

Instruction is Limited and Constrained

In Krashen's theoretical framework called the Monitor Theory (Krashen, 1982), Krashen argued that instruction plays a limited role in second language acquisition. Krashen's ideas on learning are that learners acquire language through interaction with language, most notably through comprehension of the input they are exposed to. Acquisition is an unconscious and implicit process, and learners acquire L2 by being exposed to comprehensible input rather than learning grammar consciously through explicit grammatical rules (Krashen, 2009).

In addition to the limited role assigned to grammar instruction, Krashen also argued that L2 learners acquired grammatical features of a target language in a predictable order and this was regardless of their first language or the context in which they acquired them. In English, for example, progressive -*ing* is acquired before regular past tense -*ed*, which is acquired before third-person -*s*. His view is supported by a number of studies called 'the morpheme studies' (Dulay and Burt, 1974; Larsen-Freeman, 2000). Therefore, we might conclude that instruction might be unable to alter the route of acquisition.

In Pienemann's theoretical framework (1998), called Processability Theory, he argued that L2 learners acquire single structures through predictable stages. According to Processability Theory, instruction is constrained by these developmental stages, and L2 learners follow a very rigid route in the acquisition of grammatical structures. His position is supported by a number of studies which have found developmental sequences for a number of structures (i.e. negation, question formation) and in a number of languages (e.g. German, English, Italian, and Japanese; see Pienemann, 1984, 1987; De Biase and Kawaguchi, 2002).

The acquisition of some grammatical features seems to follow predetermined developmental stages and therefore the role of instruction is limited and constrained by L2 learners' readiness to acquire a particular structure.

Instruction is Beneficial

Many scholars have agreed that some level of attention is necessary for learning the linguistic properties of a second language. Schmidt (1990) has argued that L2 learners require conscious awareness of linguistic forms for effective processing to take place. Ellis (1994) suggested that there is some evidence to support the thesis that instruction helps L2 learners to develop greater language proficiency particularly if opportunities for natural exposure are given. He also argued that instruction has a facilitative role when it is used for linguistic features that are not too distant from the learner's current level of language development. Gass (1997) has affirmed that instruction might help learners to pay selective attention to form and form-meaning connections in the input. VanPatten (1996, 2002, 2004) has indicated that L2 learners find it difficult to attend to form and meaning simultaneously with the input they receive. Therefore, learners should be taught how to process input more effectively and efficiently so that they can process grammatical forms and connect them with their meanings.

These positions are based on the assumption that the route to acquisition cannot be altered; however, instruction might in certain conditions speed up the rate of acquisition. The two main questions are: What are the conditions that might facilitate the speed in which languages are learned? And what strategies should learners be taught?

As pointed out by VanPatten and Benati (2010: 51),

> learners bring to the task of acquisition a variety of internal mechanisms and traits which effectively override most instructional efforts. However, the more researchers learn about what learners

do with input and how they do it, the closer they come to understanding the possibilities of instructional effects. To this end, the question about the role of instruction has begun to shift in research.

Overall, research investigating the role of 'focus on form' (Doughty and Williams, 1998; Norris and Ortega, 2000) in second language acquisition has indicated the need for a grammar component in second language teaching. The question is: How should we provide this component?

The Pendulum Swing

There has been a dramatic shift from traditional grammar-oriented methods and to more recent communicative grammar techniques and approaches to second language teaching. This shift has meant a change in the way grammar is taught and practised in the language classroom.

In the Grammar Translation Method, an explicit approach to grammar teaching was proposed. One of the main assumptions of this methodology was that a second language is learned through the deduction of the grammatical properties of L2 and this would allow learners to develop a conscious and explicit representation of that language in their internal system. Grammar instruction consisted mainly of studying forms and structures with memorization and translation of texts.

The Direct Method introduced a more inductive view of the role of grammar instruction. According to this method, L2 learners should learn grammar by interpreting contextual and situational cues rather than receiving explicit information about the new language. However, the focus of grammar instruction was still on learning the grammatical properties of the L2 and not developing any communication skills.

The Audio-lingual Method suggested that grammar is learned through the process of repetition, imitation and reinforcement. Grammatical structures were presented in a linear manner with no attention to meaning. This method emphasized the use of memorization and pattern drills as grammar teaching tasks.

Another grammar-based approach which represents a traditional way of providing grammar instruction is called PPP (presentation, practice, production). This approach proposed a three-stage model. The first stage consisted of the internalization of a new form or structure which is usually presented through a text. The second stage implies the practice of the new form of structure through its systematic use. In the final stage, activities are organized involving personal use of the target form or structure. The PPP suggests the use of activities which allow the learner to move from systematic to appropriate use of the language in contexts. It is only when the student has mastered the form that s/he will be able to use it in context where the message becomes more important than the medium.

Grammar teaching was relegated to a fragile and peripheral role in the Natural Approach and in Communicative Language Teaching. In Communicative Language Teaching, it was assumed that grammar teaching does not help learners develop any kind of communicative ability in the L2. It was believed that the process of learning a second language is just like learning a first language.

In the Communicative Language Teaching and Task-based Instruction approach, learners are asked to perform tasks with large quantities of meaning-focused input that contain target forms and vocabulary. The main purpose of Communicative Language Teaching is to develop learners' ability to interpret and use meaning in real-life communication and not focus on the learning of forms and structures. However, both approaches have attempted to incorporate a component of grammar instruction within an overall focus on communication.

Focus on Form and Focus on Forms

Long (1991) distinguished between two types of grammar instruction approaches: 'focus on form' and 'focus on forms'. More recently he provided a clear definition of these two terms (Long and Robinson, 1998): 'focus on forms' refers to a type of instruction that isolates specific linguistic forms, and teaches them one at a time. In this traditional approach, grammar instruction is often characterized by paradigmatic explanations of specific linguistic forms or structures (see example below).

> There are four types of pronouns: Subject Pronouns, Object Pronouns, Possessive Pronouns and Demonstrative Pronouns. **Object Pronouns – me, you, him, her, it, us, you, them –** serve as the object of a verb. Object pronouns are used instead of object nouns, usually because we already know what the object is.
> He told **you** to come tonight.
> She asked **him** to help.
> They visited **her** when they came to New York.
> She bought **it** at the store.
> He picked **us** up at the airport.

The teacher asked **you** to finish your homework.
I invited **them** to a party.

Singular	Plural
Me	Us
You	You
Him	Them
Her	
It	

The paradigmatic explanation is followed by pattern practice and substitution drills (see below). In this type of mechanical practice, real-life situations are completely ignored and practice is implemented in a completely decontextualized way (see Wong and VanPatten, 2003).

Change the sentence, substituting object pronouns in place of the direct object

a.   John put the glasses on the table
     John put **them** on the table
b.   John put the forks on the table
     John put_____ on the table

The idea that acquiring grammar can be achieved simply by learning about the grammatical rules of a target language and practising those rules through production tasks (very often mechanical and traditional) has been challenged by many scholars in the field of second language acquisition and language teaching.

In recent years, findings from empirical research in instructed second language acquisition and theory have demonstrated that a component of focus on grammar ('focus on form') might facilitate acquisition if it is provided in combination with a focus on meaning. The term 'focus on form' is characterized by techniques which provide a focus on meaning and a focus on form. In grammar teaching techniques under the term 'focus on form', learners' attention is being focused on specific linguistic properties in the course of a communicative task. Spada (1997: 73) has defined more broadly 'focus on form' as 'any pedagogical effort which is used to draw learners' attention to language form either implicitly or explicitly'. A series of pedagogical options to grammar teaching under the umbrella of 'focus on form' will now be examined.

Input-based Options to Grammar Teaching

Input plays a key role in second language acquisition. Its centrality has been emphasized by many theories (e.g. Universal Grammar, Interaction Hypothesis, Input Processing) and scholars (White, 2003; Gass, 1997; VanPatten, 1996). Gass (1997: 1) has defined input as 'the single most important concept in second language acquisition'. Considering the limited role for instruction, and the importance of incorporating grammar in a more communicative framework of language teaching, teachers should look at devising grammar tasks that, on one hand, enhance the grammatical features in the input, and on the other hand, provide L2 learners with opportunities to focus on meaning. The question is to determine what type of grammar is more successful in terms of helping learners internalize the grammatical features of a target language.

In this section, the following input-based approaches to grammar instruction will be considered:

- − processing instruction, and
- − input enhancement techniques.

Processing instruction

In traditional grammar instruction L2 learners are provided with explicit information about a particular target form or structure, and this is followed by mechanical practice. Unlike traditional instruction, where the focus of instruction is in the manipulation of learners' output, processing instruction aims at changing the way input is perceived and processed by L2 learners. Processing instruction is an input-based approach to grammar instruction predicated on *Input processing theory* (VanPatten, 1996, 2002, 2004; VanPatten and Jegerski, 2010). Input processing refers to the fact that language learners are exposed to input which contains linguistic forms. When L2 learners process input, they have limited resources to ensure that they make correct form-meaning connections. When they hear a sentence such as 'I talked to my teacher' and understand that 'talked' means that the action is in the past, a form-meaning connection is made. They cannot just notice the form, as they need to comprehend the meaning that the particular form encodes. VanPatten (1996) has identified two main processing strategies that learners might use when they are exposed to language input. According to the Primacy of Meaning Principle, learners will first process input for meaning before they process the linguistic form. The result of this will be that learners will not make natural connections between forms in the input and their meanings.

According to the First Noun Principle, learners will tend to process the first noun or pronoun they encounter in a sentence as the subject or agent. The result of this will be that learners will misinterpret sentences in which the first element in a sentence is not the subject or agent (e.g. passive constructions).

Processing instruction aims at altering the processing strategies/principles that 'learners take to the task of comprehension and to encourage them to make better form-meaning connections than they would if left to their own devices' (Van Patten, 1996: 60). Processing instruction is an input-based option to grammar instruction which guides L2 learners to focus on small parts/features of the targeted language when they process the input. Its characteristics have been described in detail in previous literature (Van-Patten, 1996; Lee and VanPatten, 1995, 2003; Farley, 2005, Wong, 2004, 2005; Lee and Benati, 2007a, 2007b, Benati and Lee, 2008, Lee and Benati, 2009, Benati and Lee, 2010). Processing instruction consists of two main components: explicit information and structured input practice.

The first component is the explicit information component. Learners are given explicit information about a linguistic structure or form. Forms or structures are presented one at a time, e.g. regular past forms, passive constructions. The information is used to alert L2 learners of possible processing problems. L2 learners are given information on a particular processing principle that may negatively affect their picking up the form or structure during comprehension. The explicit information provided should help L2 learners to be aware of this processing problem when they process input.

The second component is the structured input practice component. After receiving explicit information, learners are pushed to process the form or structure through structured input activities. In structured input activities the input is manipulated in particular ways to make learners become dependent on form and structure to get meaning. As outlined by Wong (2004: 35), processing instruction 'pushes learners to abandon their inefficient processing strategies for more optimal ones so that better form-meaning connections are made'.

Van Patten and Sanz (1995) originally produced the following guidelines for developing structured input activities:

a. Present one thing at a time.
b. Keep meaning in focus.
c. Move from sentences to connected discourse.
d. Use both oral and written input.
e. Have the learner do something with the input.
f. Keep the learner's processing strategies in mind.

Wong (2004: 37) has emphasized that 'for an activity to be a structured input activity, that activity must somehow push learners to circumvent an inefficient processing strategy'. Identifying the processing problem in a target language is the most important step in developing structured input activities. We can see how guidelines developed by VanPatten and Sanz (1995) can be applied when we develop structured input practice.

a. Rules should be broken down into smaller parts and taught one at a time during the course of the lesson. Learners are presented with the linguistic feature before being exposed to structured input activities. We should avoid providing L2 learners with lots of information and grammatical rules as learners possess a limited capacity for processing information. Presenting L2 learners with a smaller and more focused amount of information will clearly enhance the opportunity for learners to pay more focused attention.

b. Keeping meaning in focus is crucial when we develop structured input activities. Tasks in structured input activities must be completed with focused attention to the referential meaning of the input to which L2 learners are exposed. A good structured input activity is one where students must understand the meaning of the sentence to complete the task. In order to complete the task and express their opinions L2 learners must understand the meaning of each utterance.

c. L2 learners are first exposed to sentences and at a later stage they should be provided with connected discourse. This should happen only when learners have already had opportunities to process the new form or structure.

d. Structured input activities which combine oral and written input should be used because there are different types of learners. This is in order to account for individual differences. In addition, as noticed by Farley (2005: 15), 'hearing the forms allow only for sound-meaning connections, whereas written form-meaning connections are made via reading'.

e. Structured input activities should be designed to make learners do something with the input they receive (i.e. agreeing or disagreeing; false or true; likely or unlikely). During structured input activities L2 learners should be encouraged to make form-meaning connections. Learners must engage in processing the input (having a specific reason for processing input) and must respond to the input sentence in some way.

f. Learners' attention should be guided so as not to rely on natural processing strategies. Activities in which the input is structured to alter learners' reliance on one particular processing principle should be created. This is the main goal for structured input activities: correcting inefficient processing strategies and instilling in L2 learners more efficient ones. Structured input activities are of two types: referential and affective. Referential activities (see Activity 2.1) are those where there is a right or wrong answer and where the learner must rely on the targeted grammatical form to get meaning.

Activity 2.1 Referential structured input

Things people did now and last summer
Listen to the following statements and decide whether each statement refers to an activity that takes place now or took place last summer in London.

     NOW   LAST SUMMER

1   ☐   ☐

2   ☐   ☐

(the activity continues in similar fashion)

Sentences heard by learners:

1. People handed out bread to the pigeons at Trafalgar Square.
2. People protest in London about the war.

Affective structured input activities are those in which learners express an opinion, belief, or some other affective response and are engaged in processing information about the real world (see Activity 2.2). Learners might be asked to express an opinion or view about something. Learners must be engaged in processing the input sentences and must respond to the input sentence in some way through referential and affective types of structured input activities.

Activity 2.2 Affective structured input

How well do you know your teacher?
Select the phrase that best completes each statement about your teacher.
Afterward, we will tell you if you are correct or not.

1. As soon as he gets home, my teacher...

a. reads the mail
b. plays with his kids
c. has a glass of wine

2. When it is time for dinner, he...

a. prepares the meal
b. helps with the meal
c. orders a pizza

(the activity continues in similar fashion)

Processing instruction is an instructional technique which, through the manipulation and restructuring of the input, might help learners to acquire grammatical and syntactic features of a target language.

Input enhancement techniques

✸Scholars in second language acquisition have agreed that L2 learners must be exposed to input and that input must be comprehensible and meaning-bearing in order to facilitate the L2 acquisition. Krashen (1982) has argued that conscious learning has no effects on the ability of L2 learners to acquire a second language in spontaneous communication. Schmidt (1990) has suggested that L2 learners require attention in order to process successfully forms in the input. Learners must first notice a form in the input for that form to be processed. Given the importance of 'noticing' a form in the input the question is: how can we best facilitate the noticing of a certain form in the input? Input enhancement has been defined by Sharwood-Smith (1991) as a process by which linguistic data will become more salient for L2 learners. This form of intervention (enhancing the input to allow learners to notice some specific forms in the input) should effect changes in learners' linguistic competence. Sharwood-Smith (1991) has proposed various techniques to enhance the input which varies in terms of explicitness and elaboration. A practical example would be to underline or to capitalize a specific grammatical item in a text to help learners notice that particular grammatical feature (textual enhancement). A different technique would be to modify a text so that a particular target item appears over and over again; in this way the text would contain many more exemplars of the same feature (input flood).

Input enhancement is an approach to grammar instruction through which input is made more noticeable to the L2 learner. Input enhancement techniques help teachers to expose learners to comprehensible input and positive evidence while at the same time drawing learners' attention to some linguistic properties of the target language. The target form is enhanced by visually altering (see Activity 2.3) its appearance in the text (using italics, bold, underline). Oral input enhancement can also be provided by using special stress, intonation and gestures in spoken input.

Activity 2.3 Textual enhancement

> Bill **goes** to the cinema every weekend. He **likes** Aldomóvar and Tarantino films. Sometimes he **plays** tennis with his friends or **goes** to the gym. On Saturday, he **works** at the University and sometimes he **takes** the car and **drives** to the countryside.
>
> (Text continues)
>
> Follow-up: What kind of things do you like to do at the weekend? What type of things do you have to do?

Designing input enhancement tasks will involve following these guidelines:

a)   choose a grammatical feature that learners need to pay attention to;
b)   highlight the feature in the text using a textual enhancement technique (e.g. bold, underline);
c)   keep learners' attention on meaning;
d)   do not provide any metalinguistic explanation.

The form has been highlighted in the dialogue (see Activity 2.3) with the use of a textual enhancement technique in the hope that learners will notice it. The advantages of this textual enhancement activity are listed as follows (Wong, 2005: 56):

1. Learners can be exposed to more instances of the target form, therefore there is a greater likelihood that they will notice the form.
2. Learners will be exposed to meaning-bearing input from this type of task.
3. It is a form of input enhancement that can be easily integrated and it is easy to use.

As Wong (2005: 37) has affirmed, in input flood 'the input learners received is saturated with the form that we hope learners will notice and possibly acquire. We do not usually highlight the form in any way to draw attention to it nor do we tell learners to pay attention to the form [see Table 2.4]. We merely saturate the input with the form'. When we design input flood activities we should follow these guidelines (Wong, 2005: 44):

a) grammatical tasks using input flood should either be used in written or oral input;
b) the input learners receive must be modified so that it contains many instances of the same form/structure;
c) input flood must be meaningful and learners must be doing something with the input (i.e. reconstruct a story, draw a picture).

The main purpose of designing input flood activities is to expose learners to a greater amount of input (through this technique) containing the target form (past tense is enhanced by increasing frequency) which will allow learners to notice and subsequently acquire this form (see Activity 2.4). As pointed out by Wong (Wong, 2005: 43) overall advantages of input flood are:

1) input flood material can be accommodated easily to any subject in which learners are interested;
2) the instructor can simply manipulate any materials so that this input contains many uses of a particular target form.

The main advantage of input flood is that it provides comprehensible meaning-bearing input. It is also effective as it does not disrupt the flow of communication (Wong, 2005: 42). However, as underscored by Wong (2005: 43), 'because this technique is so *implicit*, it is difficult for instructors to know whether learners are actually learning anything through the flood'.

Activity 2.4 Input flood

Last Saturday, Richard jumped out of bed at 8 am. He poured himself three strong cups of coffee to wake up fully. He watched TV and slowly felt more awake. He wanted to go back to sleep again, but he remembered that he had to work on Saturdays. He worked part-time at Starbucks café and the manager was very strict. He walked quickly to the bus stop, but unfortunately there was a lot of traffic and so he waited for over an hour. He eventually arrived late and his manager was extremely angry. He shouted at him and said he was a useless employee. Things got worse when Richard spilled a customer's coffee all over the floor and his boss got really angry and informed him that he was sacked. Finally, Richard returned home feeling miserable and exhausted. What a horrible Saturday. At least he could sleep in on Sunday!

(Text continues)

Follow-up: After you hear the text, in pairs, give as many details as you can remember about Richard's horrible day. The group with the most details wins. You have three minutes.

Structured-based Focused Options

According to Sharwood-Smith (1991), making certain features salient in the input might help to draw learners' attention to that specific feature. Enhancing the input through different techniques might be sufficient in helping learners to pay attention to the formal properties of a targeted language without the need for metalinguistic discussion. Rutherford and Sharwood-Smith (1991) coined the term 'consciousness raising' to refer to external attempts to drawn learners' attention to formal properties of a target language.

Consciousness raising

The goal of this approach is to make learners conscious of the rules that govern the use of particular language forms while providing the opportunity to engage in meaningful interaction. During consciousness raising tasks, learners develop explicit knowledge about how the target language works and are pushed to negotiate meaning. Explicit knowledge should help learners notice that form in subsequent communicative input, while negotiation of meaning (interaction) can expose learners to more comprehensible input. During consciousness raising activities, L2 learners are encouraged to discover the rules in consciousness raising. They are provided with some data and then asked to arrive (through some tasks) at an explicit understanding of some linguistic property of the target language. Raising consciousness about a particular form enables learners to notice it in communicative input. There is a clear distinction between traditional grammar instruction and consciousness raising. As noted by Ellis (1997: 160), traditional practice is production-based whereas the main aim of a consciousness raising approach to grammar instruction is 'to construct a conscious representation of the target feature and to this end any production of the feature will be strictly limited and incidental'. The most important of these differences is that in the consciousness raising approach greater attention is paid to the form-meaning relationship while there is an attempt to situate grammatical structure and elements in questions within a broader discourse context. With this approach there is an attempt to equip the learner with an understanding of a specific grammatical feature, thereby developing a declarative rather than procedural knowledge (see Rutherford, 1987; Rutherford and Sharwood-Smith, 1988). In the case of a consciousness raising task (see Activity 2.5), L2 learners are provided with some language data and are required to provide an explicit representation of the target linguistic feature.

Activity 2.5 Consciousness raising task

Step 1
What is the difference in meaning between sentence a and sentence b? What do you think the speaker means?

a)   I was hitting my head against the wall.
b)   I hit a car at 40 miles per hour.

Step 2
Complete the sentences using your own words. What is the difference in meaning between the sentences.
a)   I was working.....
b)   I worked.....

a)   I was talking
b)   I talked....

Consciousness raising tasks should be designed with the following guidelines in mind (see Ellis, 1991 and adapted example in Activity 2.6):

    a) the task focuses on a source of difficulty for second language learners;
    b) the data provided are adequate to make learners discover the rule;
    c) the task requires minimal production on the part of the learner;

d) there is an opportunity for applying the rule to construct a personal statement in order to promote its storage as explicit knowledge.

Activity 2.6 Consciousness raising task

Step 1
Here is some information about when three people joined the company they now work for and how long they have been working there.

Name	Date joined	Length of time
Ms Regan	1945	45 years
Mr Bush	1970	20 years
Ms Thatcher	1899	9 months
Mr Baker	1990 (Feb)	10 days

Step 2
Study these sentences about these people. When is 'for' used and when is 'since' used?

a) Ms Regan has been working for her company for most of her life.
b) Mr Bush has been working for his company since 1970.
c) Ms Thatcher has been working for her company for nine months.
d) Mr Baker has been working for his company since February.

Step 3
Which of the following sentences are ungrammatical? Why?

a) Ms Regan has been working for her company for 1945.
b) Mr Bush has been working for his company for twenty years.
c) Ms Thatcher has been working for her company since 1989.
d) Mr Baker has been working for his company since 10 days.

Step 4
Try and make up a rule to explain when 'for' and 'since' are used.

Output-based Approaches to Grammar Teaching

In this section, output-based options to grammar instruction will be considered. Input plays an essential role in second language acquisition. As claimed by VanPatten and Benati (2010: 36), 'most people agree that input is necessary for acquisition, what is less clear is the role that output plays'.

The role of output in second language acquisition has been considered from two main perspectives: skill building hypothesis and comprehensible output hypothesis. From the skill building hypothesis perspective, L2 learners should first learn rules or items consciously and then gradually automatize them through practice. From a comprehensible output perspective, Swain (1985, 1995) has proposed a different role for output. According to Swain, comprehensible input is not sufficient for developing native-like grammatical competence. L2 learners need opportunities for *pushed output* (speech or writing that demands learners to produce language correctly and appropriately). Swain has proposed that output contributes to L2 acquisition in three ways:

- *Hypothesis testing.* L2 learners have the opportunity to test out their hypotheses about how they express their meaning in a second language. Learners may use language production as a way of trying out new language forms and structures as they stretch their interlanguage. They may use their output to test what works and what does not.
- *Noticing.* L2 learners have the opportunity to notice a gap in their linguistic ability. The activity of producing the target language may prompt second language learners to recognize consciously some of their linguistic problems.
- *Metalingusitic function.* L2 learners have the opportunity to reflect consciously on the target language. Metatalk produced in the context of making meaning may serve the function of deepening learners' awareness of forms and rules and the relationship of those forms and rules to the meaning they're trying to express.

Skehan (1996) has also proposed a series of possible contributions for output:

- Output generates better input. L2 learners have the opportunity to negotiate meaning and provide input for somebody else.
- Output promotes syntactic processing. L2 learners have the opportunity to pay attention to the means by which meaning is expressed.
- Output helps learners in their hypothesis about grammar. L2 learners have the opportunity to try out hypotheses.
- Output helps the development of discourse skills. L2 learners have the opportunity to move from sentence to discourse production.

Considering the various roles that output can have in second language learning, we need to look at various collaborative output tasks (e.g. dictogloss, jigsaw tasks, problem-solving tasks) that might help L2 learners in acquiring the grammatical properties of an L2. Pushing L2 learners to produce output through collaborative tasks might facilitate the accurate and appropriate use of language forms and structures.

Dictogloss

Dictogloss is a type of task-based collaborative output which aims at helping learners to use their grammar resources to reconstruct a text and become aware of their own shortcomings and needs. It consists of a listening phase and a reconstruction phase where L2 learners are asked to reconstruct a text rather than write down the exact words that are dictated. As the text is read at a natural speed, students cannot write down every word, only key words, and they have to understand the meaning and use their knowledge of grammar in order to reconstruct it. Wajnryb (1990) has outlined that the dictogloss procedure consists of four stages:

a) *Preparation*: when L2 learners are informed about the topic of the text and through a series of warm-up discussions they are given the necessary vocabulary to cope with the task. It is at this stage that they are also organized into groups.

b) *Dictation*: when L2 learners hear the text for the first time at natural speed. The first time they do not take any notes. The second time, L2 learners are asked to note down key words to help them remember the content and reconstruct the text.

c) *Reconstruction*: when L2 learners work together in small groups to reconstruct the text with correct grammar and content.

d) *Analysis and correction*: when L2 learners analyse, compare and correct their texts. This is achieved with the help of the teacher and the other groups.

Dictogloss is a very effective technique for a number of reasons: learners are encouraged to focus their attention on form and meaning and all four language skills are practised; learners develop a need for communication and for group work; learners can monitor and adjust their interlanguage; learners have ample opportunity for discussion and negotiation.

In the example below (Activity 2.7) learners are encouraged to monitor and reflect on grammatical properties of the new language.

Activity 2.7 Dictogloss

Step 1
Listen to the text and make a note of as many words as you can.

Step 2
Compare your notes with your partner and try to reconstruct the text. Please check carefully for spelling and grammatical accuracy.

Step 3
Compare your version of the text with another pair, and note similarities and differences.

Similar   Different

Jigsaw task

In a jigsaw collaborative output task, L2 learners can work in pairs or in small groups. Each pair or group has different information and they have to exchange their information to complete the task. Jigsaw tasks consist of the following procedure:

- a pair of learners or a group is each given a partially completed text/chart/passage. The text includes a cloze component, which is a 'fill-in-the-blanks' activity where the learner uses clues from the context to supply words that have been deliberately removed from the text;
- one grammatical form is removed from the text (learner's version);
- learners will all have to ask the instructor to supply missing information in order to complete the task.

This type of task provides L2 learners with an opportunity to direct their attention to the target form. It also provides a great amount of negotiation as all participants have to speak and understand each other to complete the task.

In a typical jigsaw task below, L2 learners are asked to work in pairs. They each have different information and they have to give and receive information to complete a task. Each pairs are given a partially completed chart (see example in Activity 2.8) containing different information about four people (Paul, John, Sarah, Joanne). The information might be about where they come from, how many other people live in their house, how many pets they have, what their favourite sports are, and what music they like best. Learners take turns to ask and answer questions regarding the four people without looking at their partner's chart. Both partners must request and supply missing information in order to complete all the details for the four people.

Activity 2.8 Jigsaw task chart

	Paul	John	Sarah	Joanne
Nationality				American
Number of people in the house			2	
Number of pets		4		
Favourite sport	Tennis			
Favourite music			Rock	

Structured output tasks

Structured output tasks are an effective alternative to mechanical output practice. As stated by Lee and VanPatten (1995: 121), structured output activities have two main characteristics: '(1) They involve the exchange of previously unknown information; and (2) They require learners to access a particular form or structure in order to process meaning'. In the example below (see Activity 2.9) the focus is on one form and one meaning and learners have to respond to the content of the output.

Activity 2.9 Structured output task

Step 1
Indicate if you do each of the following activities *often* or *rarely*.

Activities	Often	Rarely
Play football		
Go swimming		
Eat out		
Read a book		
Listen to music		

Step 2
Using the information from step 1, create a series of questions to ask your classmate during an interview.

> **Step 3**
> Interview your classmate.
>
> **Step 4**
> Prepare a set of statements in which you compare what you do and what your classmate does using the ideas from steps 1, 2 and 3. You will present your results to the class and after you have received feedback from other classmates you will draw some conclusions about the student's habits.

Conclusion

Traditional grammar instruction is not an appropriate way of approaching the teaching of grammatical forms and the structure of a second language. Paradigmatic explanation of a grammatical rule followed by mechanical and meaningful drill practice is not an effective way to focus on form in the language classroom. However, there are types of 'focus on form' approaches to grammar instruction that can in certain cases and conditions enhance and speed up the way languages are learned and are an effective way to incorporate grammar teaching and grammar tasks in communicative language teaching. Input enhancement techniques provide foreign language learners with access to comprehensible input, positive evidence and help L2 learners to pay attention to grammatical forms in the input. Processing instruction and structured input practice helps learners to process input correctly and efficiently and therefore increases learners' intake and provides the correct information for learners. Consciousness raising tasks help learners to pay attention to grammatical forms in the input while at the same time provide the necessary input learners need to acquire a L2. Collaborative output tasks are useful tasks as they provide L2 learners with an opportunity to produce output, promote negotiation of form and at the same time develop learners' linguistic skills.

Here are some of the principles that language instructors should take into account when developing grammar tasks and providing grammar instruction in the language classroom:

- given that acquisition can be effectively influenced by manipulating input, grammar tasks should be developed to ensure that learners process input correctly and efficiently;
- grammar tasks should be designed for learners to notice and process forms in the input and eventually make correct form-meaning connections;

- language teaching should include a variety of grammar tasks that invite both a focus on form and a focus on meaning;
- language teaching should include grammar tasks which apply to all learner types;
- considering the role of output in second language acquisition, collaborative output tasks should be used to promote language production and the development of grammatical skills.

According to Nassaji and Fotos (2011: 139),

> teachers should be eclectic in their pedagogical approach. That is, they should choose and synthesize the best elements, principles and activities of different approaches to grammar teaching to attain success. Thus, not only do teachers have to maximize opportunities for the students to encounter important target forms in communicative contexts, they also need to be flexible and use a variety of means to do so.

Suggested Reading

Benati, A., and Lee, J. F. (2008). *Grammar Acquisition and Processing Instruction: Secondary and Cumulative Effects.* Clevedon: Multilingual Matters.

This volume provides a good introduction to the processing instruction approach with many examples of structured input activities. The book also presents the results of classroom-based empirical research that investigates primary and secondary effects of processing instruction.

Nassaji, H., and Fotos, S. (2011). *Teaching Grammar in Second Language Classrooms.* New York: Routledge.

This text, designed specifically for language teachers, presents and examines the various options in grammar teaching. It provides a clear and easy description of each option, their theoretical and empirical background, and guidelines for developing and implementing each grammar option in the classroom.

Wong, W. (2005). *Input Enhancement: From Theory and Research to the Classroom.* New York: McGraw-Hill.

This book provides teachers with a review of various grammar techniques in grammar teaching (e.g. input enhancement, processing instruction, consciousness raising). Each chapter provides the reader with a description of each technique and how the technique can be carried out.

3 Key Issues in Interactional and Corrective Feedback

Chapter Preview

In this chapter, different corrective feedback techniques to provide L2 learners with a focus on form through interactional feedback will be proposed.

Key approaches to interaction and corrective feedback are based on the assumption that negotiated interaction is a key element in second language learning and teaching.

Introduction

The role of interactional and corrective feedback is a key issue in second language acquisition. Interaction refers to conversations between learners and other interlocutors (e.g. native speakers and non-native speakers, learner–teacher interactions). Very often the input of one speaker is modified by another speaker and this is normally due to lack of comprehension (What did you say? Do you mean *tonight*? Sorry?) and a breakdown in communication. Corrective feedback refers to utterances from a language instructor or another speaker which indicates that the learner's output is not correct. This term is often interchanged with the term 'negative evidence' which relates to different techniques used to alert L2 learners what is not possible in a second language. VanPatten and Benati (2010: 114) have made a clear distinction between direct and indirect negative evidence.

Direct negative evidence refers to feedback in which the learner is explicitly told his or her utterance is incorrect in some way. Indirect negative evidence refers to different forms of implicit corrective feedback using various forms of reformulation, modification and negotiation strategies. Conversational interaction between native speakers (NS) and non-native speakers (NNS) can facilitate language development (see example below).

NS: How did you come to school?
NNS: Bike.
NS: I also ride a bike.
NNS: Yes, I ride a bike.

The *Interaction Hypothesis* (Long, 1996; Gass, 1997) focuses on how such interactions might affect language acquisition.

In this chapter, we examine the role of interactional modifications and corrective feedback in language learning and language teaching. It is through negotiation of meaning that L2 learners not only resolve break-down in communication and clarify somebody else's message, but also receive corrective feedback on erroneous sentences. The feedback should be provided though different conversational techniques (e.g. clarification requests, confirmation checks, repetition, recasts, etc.) during interaction and classroom tasks. In the past thirty years, the key issues addressed by scholars and researchers are:

- Should errors be corrected?
- How should we correct errors?
- Who should do the correcting?
- When should we correct errors?

Key Aspects

Various types of interactional feedback will be presented in this chapter. The classification used by Nassaji and Fotos (2011) between reformula-tion and elicitation to distinguish two types of interactional feedback will be adopted. Reformulations are those corrective feedback techniques such as recasts. Recasts refer to an implicit technique to corrective feedback in which L2 learners are provided with the correct form immediately after their erroneous utterance. The correction is implicit and incidental. How-ever, there are different forms for providing learners with a signal that there is 'something wrong' in their output. Elicitations, for example, refer to others' corrective feedback techniques which do not provide L2 learn-ers with the correct form. Repair techniques such as clarification requests and elicitations do not provide the correct target form. Learners are encour-aged to repair their own errors by providing them with a prompt and thus a chance to reformulate their utterances.

An interactional modification such as a comprehension check or a request for clarification between instructor and learner or one learner and another learner during communication occurs through a process called *negotiation of meaning*.

Key Developments

The role of interactional corrective feedback has been investigated in instructed second acquisition research. One line of research has investigated the role of conversational interaction between NS and NNS. This line of research has established the importance of negotiation of meaning and negative feedback.

As indicated by many scholars, input is a key and vital ingredient in second language acquisition (Gass, 1997; VanPatten and Williams, 2007). However, in order to be effective it must be comprehended by the learner and it must have a communicative intent. The *Interaction Hypothesis* recognizes the importance of comprehensible input, and views interactional modifications as crucial in making input comprehensible. Classroom research has proved that more interactional modifications and negotiation takes place in paired group activities than teacher-fronted activities. Negotiation has been defined by Lee (2000) as 'interactions during which speakers come to terms, reach agreements, make arrangements, solve a problem or settle an issue by conferring or discussing'.

Long (1996) argues that negotiation of meaning has a facilitative role in second language acquisition because it does engage learners at input and output level. Pica (1994) assigns to the negotiation of meaning two main roles. First of all, negotiation of meaning is, according to Pica, helping L2 learners to comprehend the message contained in the input. Secondly, it facilitates the production of modified output after L2 learners receive feedback on their erroneous output.

The role of negative feedback is closely related to the role of focus on form presented and examined in the previous chapter. Doughty and Williams (1998) define a 'focus on form' as any type of instruction that encourages focus on meaning and a focus on form at the same time. Focus on form can include an instructional intervention that seeks to attract learners' attention to formal features of a L2 within a meaningful context or a reaction to errors (corrective negative feedback). Spada (1997) has argued that focus on form is generally more beneficial when L2 learners' attention is drawn to linguistic features in an implicit way within a communicative teaching context. Long (1996) argues that recast is a form of implicit negative feedback where the learner's attention is drawn to mismatches between the input and the output. Recast is a form of corrective feedback where instructors provide a correct version (correct form) of the utterance. Recast enables teachers to provide feedback without hindering L2 learners' communicative intent.

Research on negative feedback has attempted to establish whether or not corrective feedback is a necessary and/or beneficial factor for language development. Cross-sectional and longitudinal studies have been conducted to establish the effectiveness of implicit corrective feedback techniques, particularly recast techniques (see Long, 2007 for a full review of these studies). Lyster and Ranta (1997) have argued that recast is not effective in eliciting immediate revision by learners of their output. Lyster and Ranta investigated what types of error treatments encourage learners to correct their own errors (self-repair). In their data analysis they identified six different corrective feedback types:

- explicit error correction with the language instructor indicating that the learner's sentence was incorrect;
- implicit recast with no indication that the learner's sentence was incorrect;
- clarification requests with the language instructor indicating that the message has not been understood or that the learner's sentence contained an error;
- metalinguistic clues with the language instructor providing comments related to the sentence produced by L2 learners but not the correct form;
- elicitation with the language instructor eliciting the correct form from learners by asking questions, pausing or asking learners to reformulate a sentence;
- repetition.

They also identified two main types of learners' uptake (learners' reaction following language instructors' feedback): uptake that produces a new sentence still needing repair; and uptake that produces a repair of the error on which the language instructor's feedback is focused. The results from this study showed that recasts and explicit correction did not result in learner-generated repair. However, when learners were more engaged in the language process through the use of other techniques (e.g. elicitations, clarification requests), they were able to self-repair.

Lyster and Ranta (1997) concluded that corrective feedback is more effective when L2 learners are actively engaged in negotiating a form, or when they have to think about and respond to the language instructor's feedback in some way. The opportunity of negotiating forms is better achieved when the language instructor does not provide the correct form but instead provides cues to help the learner consider how to reformulate his or her incorrect language.

A second line of research has provided a more positive support for the role of recast (see Doughty and Williams, 1998). Scholars in support of recast techniques suggest that it might enable learners to be exposed to forms and elicit repetition, and this repetition may in turn enhance acquisition. Overall, the results of these studies have indicated that L2 learners benefit from the use of implicit corrective feedback in the form of recasts. Recast has a facilitative role and provides learners with a focus on form without interrupting the flow of conversation and at the same time learners can focus on message content. The role of interactional feedback is also closely associated with Schmidt's Noticing Hypothesis (1990). Developing learners' ability to notice the gap by drawing their attention to the incorrect form they have produced might help them to notice discrepancies between their interlanguage and the target language. One of the hypotheses proposed by Long and Robinson (1998) is that corrective interactional feedback (e.g. recast) can provide L2 learners with an opportunity to contrast correct and incorrect forms, by recasting the learner's utterance with the correct form.

Interactional corrective feedback can occur in two different ways: reformulations (e.g. recasts) and elicitation (e.g. clarification requests) techniques. Ellis (2009) has renamed these two interactional feedback approaches as input providing and output prompting approaches.

Recast by definition refers to a reformulation of learners' erroneous utterance into a correct form without sacrificing an overall focus on meaning. Recast is used by instructors to make sure that the speaker becomes aware that something is wrong in their speech production. Below is one example of how recast can be used (Spada and Lightbown, 1993: 76):

NNS: It bugs me when a bee sting me.
NS: Oh, when a bee stings me.
NNS: Stings me.
NS: Do you get stung often?

In the above example, the non-native speaker produces a sentence which contains an error. The native speaker (language tutor) provides a recast by reformulating the learner's incorrect form into a correct form. The successful correction made by the non-native speaker is called uptake. The native speaker continues the interaction in the attempt not to break the flow of communication. The degree of explicitness in using this technique would vary also depending on the use of intonational signals. In the example below the added stress makes the recast more explicit:

> NNS: It bugs me when a bee sting me.
> NS: Oh, when a bee STINGS me.
> NNS: Stings me.
> NS: Do you get stung often?

Recast is an interactional and implicit corrective feedback technique which can be implemented in different ways. The NS reformulated the NNS utterance with the intention to correct one or multiple errors.

Clarification requests occur when there is a breakdown of communication between two speakers. One speaker asks the other speaker to clarify his/her utterance. It does not provide the speaker with the correct form; however it gives the other speaker the opportunity for self-repair. Phrases such as 'sorry?' or 'what did you say? or 'say it again, please' provide the learner with an opportunity to clarify and/or make his utterance more accurate. Below is an example of clarification requests (from VanPatten and Benati, 2010: 11):

> NNS: I can find no [ruddish].
> NS: *I'm sorry. You couldn't find what?*

Metalinguistic feedback provides NNS with a metalinguistic cue in the input and/or metalinguistic feedback about the correctness of an utterance. The two examples below are from Nassaji and Fotos (2011: 77):

> NNS: I see him in the office yesterday.
> NS: You need a past tense (metalinguistic cue).

> NNS: He catch a fish.
> NS: Caught is the past tense (metalinguistic feedback and correction).

With direct elicitation the NS attempts to elicit relevant information from the NNS. There is no correction but an opportunity for self-repair/correction (see example below from Nassaji and Fotos, 2011: 77):

NNS: And when the young girl arrive, ah, beside the old woman.
NS: When the young girl....?

Conclusion

Four of the key questions asked by language instructors and practitioners in the context of error correction are: Should we correct errors? How should we correct errors? Who should do the correcting? When should we correct errors?

Comprehensible input is a necessary ingredient for second language acquisition; however it might not be sufficient. Corrective feedback might play a facilitative role in helping L2 learners process linguistic items of the target language in the language input they receive. The information provided to L2 learners through corrective feedback should allow them to confirm, to falsify and/or to modify their interlanguage. If we assume that errors should be corrected to provide opportunities for L2 learners to improve their competence, the question is: what form of corrective feedback is the most appropriate to facilitate acquisition? Although more classroom research is needed to fully answer this question, the empirical evidence so far on the role of corrective feedback seems to indicate that it might be more effective for L2 learners when it is provided more implicitly and when L2 learners are provided with opportunities to negotiate meaning. Based on these assumptions we can provide some ideas and suggestions for second language instructors:

- Error correction techniques that require L2 learners to reflect on language structures or vocabulary should be adopted. These types of corrective feedback elicit student-generated repairs.
- Language instructors should be eclectic in choosing an error correction technique depending on different factors (e.g. structures, levels of proficiency). Good language instructors understand that one size does not fit all. Choosing to use a different type of corrective feedback that seems to produce student-generated repairs increases chances of reaching more learners.
- Language instructors should encourage learners to self-correct. Language instructors often correct learners' responses before they have enough time to process the information. Instead they should allow learners the time to respond and provide appropriate cues for the learner to self-repair.

Suggested Reading

Doughty C., and Williams, J. (eds) (1998). *Focus on Form in Classroom Second Language Acquisition*. New York: Cambridge University Press.

> This volume presents and reviews research on the effectiveness of a focus on form in second language learning and teaching. The final chapter of this volume provides the reader with an examination of different ways in providing a focus on form in the language classroom.

Long, H. M. (2007). *Problems in SLA*. Mahwah, NJ: Lawrence Erlbaum Associates.

> Part two of this book provides an updated review and discussion on the role of implicit corrective feedback in second language acquisition.

Lyster, R., and Ranta, L. (1997). Corrective feedback and learner uptake: Negotiation of form in communicative classrooms. *Studies in Second Language Acquisition*, 19, 37–66.

> This classroom study is an investigation into the effects of different corrective feedback techniques. The main findings of this empirical study have classroom implications in supporting the effectiveness of self-repair techniques in language learning and teaching.

Sheen, Y. (2011). *Corrective Feedback, Individual Differences and Second Language Learning*. New York: Springer.

> This book provides an overview on the role of corrective feedback in language learning and teaching. This book is an important resource for students and language teachers in offering an understanding of how error correction strategies can be applied in the classroom.

4 Key Issues in the Teaching of Speaking

Chapter Preview

In this chapter, some of the key issues around the role of speaking in second language acquisition will be examined. Guidelines and principles that language instructors might follow to produce effective tasks that would help L2 learners improve their oral skills in second language learning will be offered.

An outline of the basic principles derived from theory, focusing on the notion of a 'task' as central to the teaching of speaking, will be provided.

Introduction

The ability to speak in another language is often associated with the overall main goal of learning another language. Speaking is a language process in which learners build and share meaning through the use of verbal and non-verbal symbols, and in a variety of contexts. Despite the fact that we have made advances in understanding the crucial role of speaking in second language learning and teaching, language instructors have continued to teach speaking using traditional techniques such as repetition of drills or memorization of dialogues. However, the main purpose of teaching speaking skills is to improve students' communicative competence and the ability for learners to express themselves accurately and appropriately in different situations.

A key issue in language teaching is: What is the most effective way to develop oral language ability? It is understood, and most scholars have agreed, that in order to help learners develop their oral skills, language instructors must promote and develop tasks in which L2 learners are engaged in comprehending, negotiating and expressing meaning. Language is seen as a system for the expression and negotiation of meaning and therefore language instructors' focus should be on developing meaningful activities that promote real communication between L2 learners. One of the instructor's main objectives in language teaching is promoting and developing L2 learners' communicative competence. Some of those communicative tasks proposed for teaching oral skills are based on the *information gap* principle. In order to complete the assigned task, learners must be given opportunities to exchange information and interact with each other. Other tasks are based on the so-called *role-playing* principle. In this case, each learner is given a role and a task that must be accomplished through interaction with other learners. Other oral communicative tasks are based on the assumption that L2 learners must exchange information and complete a task (exchange information task) with the information gathered. Overall, we must aim at developing oral tasks to increase L2 learners' ability to communicate for a purpose. In this chapter we review appropriate and effective ways of promoting and developing oral language skills.

Key Aspects

In order to develop their speaking abilities in another language, L2 learners need to have an adequate vocabulary, pronounce words correctly, use word and sentence stress, organize their thoughts in a meaningful and logical sequence, use the language quickly and confidently and master the syntax. However, these competences are not sufficient. Developing the ability to speak in a second language involves the development of communication skills (Bygate, 1987, 2001). Oral language and oral processing skills are different from writing and reading skills. Speaking is an interactive process of constructing meaning that involves producing, receiving and processing information. Speaking in another language is not just developing the ability to use grammar correctly and have access to vocabulary and pronounce words correctly (linguistic competence), it is also the ability to understand when, why and in what ways to produce language (communicative competence). L2 learners must be engaged in communicative tasks where they use language that is meaningful. All communicative tasks must engage learners in sharing information, negotiating meaning and interacting with others. Approaches to the teaching of oral skills must be developed with the intention of promoting communication and communicative language use. One of the key terms in this chapter is 'task'. As defined by Lee (2000: 32), 'a task is (1) a classroom activity or exercise that has (a) an objective attainable only by interaction among participants, (b) a mechanism for structuring and sequencing interaction, and (c) a focus on meaning exchange; (2) a language learning endeavour that requires learners to comprehend, manipulate and/or produce the target language as they perform some set of workplans'.

Ellis (2003: 16) has defined a task as

> a work plan that requires learners to process language pragmatically in order to achieve an outcome that can be evaluated in terms of whether the correct or appropriate propositional content has been conveyed. To this end, it requires them to give primary attention to meaning and to make use of their own linguistic resources, although the design of the task may dispose them to choose particular forms. A task is intended to result in language use that bears resemblance, direct or indirect, to the language used in the real world. Like other language activities, a task can engage productive or receptive, and oral or written skills and also various cognitive processes.

Key Developments

Linguistic competence is a necessary requirement for somebody who wants to speak in another language. However, communicative competence (Hymes, 1972) is also necessary to be able to communicate competently in a second language. Communicative competence comprises the knowledge of the grammatical system of a second language as well as the knowledge of the social and cultural contexts. Communicative language competence is made up of various components (see Figure 4.1 adapted from Bacham and Palmer, 1996). Although it appears that language ability is divided into hierarchical components of language knowledge, these components all interact with each other and with features of the language use situation. It is the interaction between knowledge and language use in context that characterizes communicative language use. Language competence involves two components: language knowledge and strategic competence. Language knowledge includes two broad categories: organizational knowledge and pragmatic knowledge. Organizational knowledge is concerned with how the utterances or sentences and texts are organized. It comprises the abilities involved in controlling the formal structure of language to produce or recognize grammatically correct sentences, understanding their content and ordering them to form texts. It is divided into grammatical knowledge (how individual utterances or sentences are organized) and textual knowledge (how utterances or sentences are organized to form texts). Grammatical knowledge includes knowledge of vocabulary, syntax, phonology and graphology. Textual knowledge (how utterances or sentences are organized to form texts) is divided into two areas: knowledge of cohesion (relationship between sentences in written texts: use of conjunction, lexical cohesion, reference) and knowledge of rhetorical conventions (how texts or conversations are organized: narration, comparison, ordering information in paragraphs, introduction, conclusion; and conversation which involves attention grabbing).

Pragmatic knowledge relates utterances or sentences and texts to their meaning, to the intentions of language users (what does s/he really want to say?) and to the general characteristics of the setting where the language is used (is it appropriate to say this in this context?). It is divided into two areas: functional knowledge and sociolinguistic knowledge. Functional knowledge enables us to understand the relationship between utterances or sentences and texts and the intentions of language users.

COMMUNICATIVE COMPETENCE

LANGUAGE COMPETENCE STRATEGIC COMPETENCE

↓ ↓ ↓ ↓ ↓

Organizational competence Pragmatic competence Goal setting Assessment Planning

↓ ↓ ↓ ↓

Grammatical Textual Functional Sociolinguistic

Figure 4.1 Communicative competence, adapted from Bacham and Palmer (1996: 66–73)

Sociolinguistic knowledge enables us to create or interpret language that is appropriate to a particular language use setting: writing a letter to a friend and writing a letter to a company, for example. This includes knowledge of the dialect, registers, natural or idiomatic expressions, and cultural references and figures of speech.

Strategic competence would include the following (see Bacham and Palmer, 1996): Goal setting (deciding what I am going to do); Assessment (what do I need to complete this task? what do I have to work with?) and Planning (how I am going to use what I know?).

Ellis (1990) reviews theory and research and extrapolates the conditions for the development of communicative competence (see also Lee, 2000):

- L2 learners must be receptive to the language and have a need and desire to communicate.
- L2 learners require opportunities to take responsibility in communication.
- Learners and instructors must make an effort to be understood (negotiation of meaning).
- L2 learners need opportunities to communicate by performing communicative functions.
- Instructors must provide learners with opportunities to participate in planned and unplanned discourse (similar to outside the classroom).
- The discourse should contain many samples of the linguistic features that learners are trying to learn.

The Interaction Hypothesis (Pica, 1994; Long, 1996; Gass, 1997; Gass and Mackey, 2007) recognizes the importance of comprehensible input (Krashen, 1982) but views interactional modifications as crucial in making input comprehensible. Classroom research has proved that interactional modifications and negotiation take place more in paired group activities than teacher-fronted activities (e.g. Doughty and Pica, 1986). Negotiation has been defined by Lee (2000: 9) as 'interactions during which speakers come to terms, reach agreements, make arrangements, solve a problem or settle an issue by conferring or discussing'. In interaction tasks the purpose of language use is to accomplish some task not to practise any particular form. Input will provide the linguistic data necessary to develop a L2 linguistic system and output will help learners develop the use of the language for communicative purposes. Developing oral language skills is to demonstrate the ability for L2 learners to accomplish pragmatic goals through interactive discourse with other speakers. Despite the fact that approaches to the teaching of oral skills are diverse, they are all based on the assumption that the main difficulty L2 learners encounter in attempting to speak is not the multiplicity of sounds, words or phrases, and discourse forms that characterize a particular second language, but rather the interactive nature of most communication.

Lee and VanPatten (2003) have emphasized that L2 learners must develop their ability to manage interaction as well as engage in the negotiation of meaning. The management of the interaction involves such things as when and how to take the floor, when to introduce a topic or change the subject, how to invite someone else to speak, how to keep a conversation going and so on. Negotiation of meaning refers to the skill of making sure the person you are speaking to has correctly understood you and that you have correctly understood them.

Oral communicative practice is antithetic to traditional oral practice largely used in traditional textbooks. In traditional oral tasks learners are asked to look at pictures or a dialogue and then perform the dialogue following a specific pattern (a typical task/exercise is: look at the pictures and practise the following patterns in the target language). Another form of a traditional oral task which is normally found in language textbooks is to ask L2 learners to talk about a topic (e.g. describe a friend or a member of your family or talk about your weekend…) without taking into consideration the main principles of the communication act and without helping L2 learners to develop communicative competence.

As described by Savignon (2005) and emphasized by Lee and VanPatten (1995: 148), the communication act involves 'the expression, interpretation and negotiation of meaning' in a given context.

Assuming that our aim is to develop L2 learners' communicative competence, we must create classroom oral tasks that stimulate communication in the language classroom. In addition to that, we must take into account practical needs and possible constraints in developing effective oral tasks. Much of the time allocated to the oral task must be occupied by learners' talk and not instructors' talk. Classroom discussion must not be dominated by a minority of talkative participants and all learners must contribute evenly (even in the case of a mixed-ability class). Oral tasks should be developed keeping learners' motivation in mind as learners are eager to speak when they interested in the topic and have something new to say about it. Learners need to use an appropriate, comprehensible and accurate level of target language. Language instructors must address some of the problems related to getting learners to talk in the classroom.

Oral tasks require some degree of real-time exposure to an audience. Learners often feel ashamed about what they are trying to say in the target foreign language in the classroom. They are often worried about making mistakes, fearful of criticism or losing face, or simply shy of the attention that their speech attracts. They often think they have nothing to say and often in group work they have very little talking time. In the language classroom, if L2 learners share the same mother tongue, they tend to use it because it is easier and feels unnatural to speak to one another in a foreign language. In traditional oral practice, instructors and learners normally exchange very little real information. Language instructors spend most of their time asking 'displayed questions' for which learners already know the answers.

Typically, an instructor asks a question (e.g. Where is the pen? Showing everybody that the pen is on the table) for which he/she and the learners know the answer, an individual learner answers, the instructor evaluates or corrects the answer, and then the cycle begins again with another learner and another question to which everyone already knows the answer. Display questions have clear limitations as, on one hand, they do not offer genuine communication practice, and on the other hand, they take learners away from the use of language for communicative purposes.

The question is: How do we provide a better approach to teaching oral skills? In adopting a principled evidence-based approach a series of measures need to be taken in order to foster the development of oral skills.

First, language instructors should develop group oral tasks which increase L2 learners' talk time and at the same time lowers the inhibitions of learners who are unwilling to speak in front of the full class. In group work, L2 learners perform a learning task through small-group interaction. One of the advantages is that it can foster learner responsibility and independence, and it can improve motivation and contribute to effective and careful organization (see Bygate, 1987).

Second, instructors should base the oral task on easy and comprehensible language that will help L2 learners to produce target language with the minimum of hesitation.

Third, language instructors should keep students speaking the target language and they should monitor the L2 learners' use of the target language at all times during their tasks. Learners should be allowed to initiate communication, and speaking tasks should involve negotiation for meaning. Positive feedback on learners' performance should be carefully provided.

Fourth, language instructors should choose an interesting and familiar topic which would enable L2 learners to use ideas from their own experience and knowledge. This step should also increase L2 learners' motivation.

Fifth, instructors should provide clear instructions to accomplish the task. Opportunities for interaction should be created (pair-group work; see Storch, 2002, 2003, 2007, 2008). If the task is based on group discussion then include instructions about participation when introducing it. For example, tell learners to make sure that everyone in the group contributes to the discussion; appoint a chairperson to each group who will regulate participation. The role of the teacher is as 'a resource person' and 'architect' as she/he structures the task but she/he is not responsible for its final accomplishment. Learners must take initiative and responsibility to complete the task. They need to make decisions in order to compete the task successfully.

Sixth, instructors should create a classroom environment where students participate in real-life communication that is authentic, and meaningful tasks that promote speaking skills. This can occur when students collaborate in groups to achieve a goal or to complete a task. L2 learners must be given a task where they have something to talk about and someone to talk to.

Seventh, language instructors should develop a task that is essentially goal-oriented and that requires the group or pair to achieve an objective that is usually expressed by an observable result, such as brief notes or lists, a rearrangement of jumbled items, a drawing, or a spoken summary. In designing a task we must make sure that learners collect data through production speech tasks designed for a specific purpose. This should be attainable only by interaction between participants. Lee (2000: 35) has indicated that in structuring an oral task, language instructors must adopt the following criteria: (a) identify a desired information outcome; (b) break down the topics into subtopics; (c) create and sequence concrete tasks for learners to do; (d) build in linguistic support. An example is provided in Activity 4.1 (exchange information task adapted from Lee and VanPatten, 2003).

In a traditional oral practice task, learners would be asked to talk about a specific topic, e.g. 'How do you spend your free time?' In this kind of task (open-ended question) learners will have very little to talk about and few opportunities to interact.

In an oral communicative practice approach, the same topic will be presented through the use of an exchange information task. In this task, learners are required to interview one of their classmates on how he/she spends his/her free time. Then, using the information they have gathered, they will make some contrastive and comparative statements.

Eighth, instructors should use a wide range of tasks to develop learners' oral skills, from conversations and interviews to role-plays, information gaps and jigsaw tasks. A role-play is a learning process in which learners act out roles in order to develop particular skills and to meet particular learning objectives.

Instructors should develop role-plays and other oral communicative tasks where learners imagine themselves in a situation outside the classroom, sometimes playing the role of someone other than themselves, and using language appropriate to this new context. Normally, the groups or pairs improvise their role-play between themselves, simultaneously, with no audience. Sometimes, however, volunteers may perform their role-plays later, in front of the class. This is one of the ways we can give L2 learners the opportunity to practise improvising a range of real-life spoken language in the classroom. In order to develop a role-play we need to identify an authentic context where learners use the target language; we need to

Step 1
Using the chart below, fill it in with at least three things that you usually do in your free time during weekdays and over the weekend. Include information about the time when you usually do these things. Use the correct verb forms to speak about yourself .

On weekdays			
On weekends			

Step 2
Now interview two people in the class with whom you have not worked much during this lesson. Ask them specific questions to find out if they do the same things. For example, if you wrote for yourself *I play football for an hour every day after class*, ask your partner 'Do you practise any sports?' and so on. The idea is to get enough information so that you can write several contrasting and comparative statements.

Step 3
Using the information obtained in steps 1 and 2 write a list of three true/false questions and three multiple-choice questions comparing and contrasting you and your classmates.

Step 4
Submit your chart and your lists to your instructor.

Activity 4.1 Exchange information task

establish authentic roles; and we need a reason to communicate and a goal/problem to resolve. Littlewood (1981: 49) has pointed out that 'in looking for ways of creating more varied forms of interaction in the classroom, teachers of foreign languages (like their colleagues in mother-tongue teaching) have turned increasingly to the field of simulation and, within that field, especially role-playing'. Role-playing is a technique which is essentially a form of simulation where learners are involved in gathering, exchanging information and communicating efficiently (see example in Activity 4.2). As Littlewood (1981: 51) argues, role-play 'gives the interaction some of the uncertainty and spontaneity involved in real communication'. Role-plays (see Savignon, 2005) aim at engaging learners in real communication in a specific social and cultural context. It is a teaching technique which requires several steps. Instructors must first choose an appropriate situation for a role-play, keeping in mind learners' needs and interests and giving them a chance to practise what they have learned.

After choosing the context (set the scene), the second step involves the design of the role-play which should take learners' level of language proficiency into consideration. In the role-play you need to generate two main roles for L2 learners. For example, in a role-play situation, at the bar, the participants have conflicting role information. One or two students have their lists of things to order while another two or three students are barmen who might not have some of the drinks, but can offer different beverages. Instructors need to provide role-players with concrete information and clear role descriptions so that they can play their roles with confidence. Learners should be provided with cards with detailed instructions (see Activity 4.2). The third step is assigning L2 learners' roles based on their proficiency

Cue Card A:

YOU ARE A TAXI-DRIVER
1. Greet the passenger and ask him where he wants to go.
2. Say the price. Make some comment on the weather. Ask the passenger if he likes this weather.
3. Answer the passenger's question. Boast that your son has won the school swimming competition. Ask if the passenger likes swimming.

Cue Card B:

YOU ARE A PASSENGER IN A TAXI
1. Greet the taxi driver and say where you want to go. Ask what the price will be.
2. Answer the taxi-driver's question and ask what kind of weather he likes.
3. Say that you like swimming a lot and that you learned to swim ten years ago when you went to Spain with your family.

Activity 4.3 Role-play

level. At the beginning level, instructors tend to take one of the roles and act it out as a model. Instructors listen to learners accomplishing role-play tasks and make notes. Only when the role-play is finished do instructors discuss with learners their experience and what they have learned. In addition to group discussion, an evaluation questionnaire can be used. Instructors provide feedback on learners' performance and praise them on their strengths, the use of language, and their acting (see another example of role-play in Activity 4.3.).

Role-play

Context – a minor car accident

Roles – Student 1 – driver of a car
Student 2 – driver of a city bus
Student 3 – police officer

Information gap (police needs information from the two drivers)
How were you driving?
Where were you going?
Where was he/she driving when he hit you?

Tasks for each role

Student 1 – very angry, tries to convince the police officer it was the bus driver's fault.
You were driving your car down the street until a bus hit you.
You are very angry.
Tell the police office that the bus driver should **get in trouble** and not you.

Student 2 – calm, thinks the car driver is stupid; of course it was her/his fault.
You were driving your bus down the street until a car suddenly **got in your way**. You are **calm** and **confident** that the car driver will get in trouble.
You think the car driver is stupid and **hot headed**.

Police Officer – thinks the bus driver's lying, impatient with car driver's attitude. You arrived at the scene of an accident between a car and a bus.
Ask both drivers these questions:
'How **were you driving**?'
'Where **were you going**?'
'Where **was he/she driving** when he/she hit you?'
'Why were you in such a hurry?'

You think the bus driver is lying. You are impatient with the car driver because he or she is too angry. You may want to **arrest** them both.

Activity 4.3 Role-play

Finally, language instructors should provide learners with oral tasks in which they must complete an information gap or solve a problem (see Pica, Karng and Sauro, 2006). Learners need to be involved in tasks where they share and process information. According to Littlewood (1981: 22) L2 learners can share and process information when they are exposed to the following types of communicative tasks: (1) tasks in which learners share information with restricted cooperation; (2) tasks in which learners share information with unrestricted cooperation; (3) tasks in which learners share and process information; (4) tasks in which learners only process information. In the first type (1) of tasks, learners must share and exchange some basic information through interaction in order to complete the task. Tasks can be designed so that one learner has to interact with another learner to discover some missing information. Learners will be working in pairs and one learner will have the information that the other learner does not have and they will have to share their information. Information-gap tasks of this kind will engage learners in tasks such as solving a problem, discovering locations, identifying pictures, finding missing information, and so on. Each learner plays an important role because the task cannot be completed if both learners do not provide the correct information. Some problem-solving tasks (see also Ur, 1981) have only one answer such as finding the quickest way to get from one place to another by car in a busy city. Another problem-solving task would involve a group of learners working together to design a list of food for sale at the school which is both healthy and appealing to students. These tasks are effective because everybody has the opportunity to talk extensively in the target language. In addition, participants learn basic strategies for requesting information or feedback. Such strategies include requesting further explanation, restating ideas, and giving additional information (e.g. What do you mean...? I can't understand you... Will you please repeat it?).

In the second type (2) of functional communication task presented by Littlewood (1981), learners are allowed to interact without restriction in order to solve the problem and complete the task. These types of task are similar to the previous one but the main purpose is to enrich communication opportunities by reducing the restricted cooperation element (e.g. storytelling, free-speaking tasks). For this activity, a teacher starts to tell a story, but after a few sentences he or she stops narrating. Then, each learner starts to narrate from the point where the previous one stopped. Each learner is supposed to add from four to ten sentences. Learners can add new characters, events, descriptions and so on. The third (3) and fourth (4) type of functional communication tasks proposed by Littlewood (1981) work on the 'jigsaw' principle. Learners work in pairs or a group and each group possesses information that is unique to the group: each group must share it with others. Together, the different pieces of information provide the material for solving a particular problem. Learners are not only asked to share information but also to discuss and evaluate specific information to complete the task.

A typical example is a task in which each member of a group needs to reconstruct the sequence of a story. One picture is given to each member of a group who will have to describe what is in the picture. The ultimate task is for learners in each group to discuss the pictures and decide on the original sequence to reconstruct the story. Another example is a task in which learners must discover differences. Learners work in pairs and each couple is given two different pictures, for example, picture of boys playing football and another picture of girls playing tennis. Students in pairs discuss the similarities and/or differences in the pictures.

Conclusion

Coming up with appropriate oral communicative tasks is a crucial factor in the development of oral skills because everything the students do is derived from the tasks and it is the tasks that generate the language to be used. Learning oral skills should be seen as a sort of partnership between instructors and L2 learners. Based on what has been presented and examined in this chapter, some ideas and suggestions which can help second language instructors to develop effective oral tasks will be provided:

- During oral tasks language instructors and learners should interact with each other. The role of the instructor is the one who designs the oral task and encourages participation and contribution from learners. The learners' role is to share responsibility in interaction and task completion. By providing a series of tasks to complete we encourage learners to take responsibility for generating the information themselves rather than just receiving it.
- Language instructors should reduce their speaking time in class and increase learners' speaking time.
- Language instructors should ask a genuine question; this is a question to which the instructor does not know the answer.
- Language instructors should provide L2 learners with opportunities to speak the target language by exposing them to a rich environment that contains collaborative work, authentic materials and tasks in which they share knowledge by interacting with each other.
- Instructors should give learners positive feedback. Instructors should indicate positive signs when commenting on a learner's performance

and should not correct learners' pronunciation mistakes very often while they are speaking.

- Teaching oral skills is a very important part of second language learning. The ability to communicate in a second language clearly and efficiently contributes to the overall success in the acquisition of a second language. Therefore, it is crucial that language instructors pay greater attention to the development of speaking skills. Rather than developing tasks leading learners to pure memorization, they should provide learners with a rich environment where meaningful communication takes place. With this main aim in mind, various speaking tasks such as those presented in this chapter (e.g. exchange information tasks, role-plays, information-gap tasks) can contribute a great deal to developing learners' communicative skills necessary in order to acquire a second language.

Suggested Reading

Bygate, M (1987). *Speaking*. Oxford: Oxford University Press.

> This book addresses the question of how L2 learners learn to speak a second language and what different approaches have been developed to teach speaking skills.

Ellis, R. (2003). *Task-Based Language Learning and Teaching*. Oxford: Oxford University Press.

> This book explores the relationship between research, teaching, and tasks. This book shows how research and task-based teaching can mutually inform each other in the development of effective language tasks.

Lee, J. (2000). *Tasks and Communicating in Language Classrooms*. New York: McGraw-Hill.

> This volume provides learners and instructors with a framework for an interactive and communicative approach to language teaching.

Lee, J., and VanPatten, B. (2003). *Making Communicative Language Teaching Happen*, 2nd edn. New York: McGraw-Hill.

> Chapter eight focuses on spoken language and information-exchange tasks. It provides readers with practical examples of how to provide learners with opportunities to communicate developing oral skills.

Littlewood, W. (1981). *Communicative Language Teaching: An Introduction*. Cambridge: Cambridge University Press.

In this volume the author provides the reader with many examples of oral communicative tasks through which L2 learners will increase their ability to convey meaning and develop oral skills.

Savignon, S (2005). *Communicative Competence: Theory and Classroom Practice*. New York: McGraw-Hill.

This is a ground-breaking text which stresses the use of meaningful language at all stages of language acquisition. It provides a framework for communicative competence which should be adhered to in developing language speaking tasks. The volume helps instructors to understand the theoretical basis for communicative language teaching and develop appropriate tasks.

5 Key Issues in the Teaching of Listening

Chapter Preview

The key issue in developing effective listening tasks is to understand the real nature of listening in another language.

In this chapter, general guidelines as to how to construct effective listening tasks in the language classroom will be presented.

An outline of the basic principles derived from theory focusing on the notion of a 'task' as central to the teaching of listening will be provided.

Introduction

One of the instructor's tasks when teaching listening is to train L2 learners to understand what is being said in a variety of listening contexts (e.g. conversation, dialogues, announcements, etc.). This is different from the case of speaking when L2 learners select the language they need and use various communicative strategies (e.g. paraphrasing) to compensate for lack of knowledge. In listening, L2 learners do not have the same control and they need to extract meaning as best as they can from the language they hear. Listeners need to be able to cope with a variety of listening situations where understanding is made difficult by a variety of factors (e.g. background noises, speed, regional accents, etc.).

Language instructors must expose learners to a selection of recorded and broadcasted materials that reflect various linguistics and situational characteristics. However, before we ask L2 learners to listen to a passage, instructors need to make sure that learners are aware of the topic they intend to focus on. This will allow them to activate their pre-existing knowledge about the specific topic and build some expectations about their listening task.

In this chapter we explore ways of providing effective listening tasks. We examine particular techniques such as brainstorming, reformulation, transformation and text expansion which have been effectively used in teaching listening skills. The key issues in developing effective listening tasks is to understand the real nature of listening in another language and developing tasks in which L2 learners are actively involved in listening to a passage for a specific purpose.

Key Aspects

Listening is one of the language skills most frequently used. L2 learners receive a great amount of information through listening from instructors and other interlocutors. Listening can be defined as an 'active skill'. Listeners are actively involved in interpreting what they hear by bringing to a listening task their own background knowledge and their linguistic knowledge to be able to process and understand the information contained in what they hear.

Learners are exposed to different listening tasks which often require different listening skills. L2 learners need to apply intentional listening; this requires the use of specific listening strategies for identifying sounds, understanding vocabulary and grammatical structures, and understanding meaning. Rost (2002) has defined listening as a process of receiving what the speaker actually says (receptive orientation); constructing and representing meaning (constructive orientation); negotiating meaning with the speaker and responding (collaborative orientation); and creating meaning through involvement, imagination and empathy (transformative orientation).

Listening involves a sender (e.g. a person, radio announcement, or television programme), a specific message, and a receiver (the listener). Listening is a very complex process in language learning as the listener needs to cope with the sender's choice of vocabulary, structure, and speed of delivery. Given the importance of listening in language learning and teaching it is essential for language instructors to help learners become effective listeners. That means that we should model listening strategies and provide listening practice in authentic situations which are likely to be encountered by L2 learners outside the classroom context.

Key Developments

The role of comprehensible input and conversational interaction has assumed greater importance in second language teaching. Krashen (1982), Gass

(1997) and Long (1996) have emphasized the benefits of providing comprehensible input, conversational interaction and negotiated interaction in the
language classroom. Considering that input is seen as a vital ingredient for
acquisition, listening is seen as a skill that has acquired an important role in
the language classroom. Language learning depends a great deal on listening
as it provides the aural input that serves as the basis for language acquisition
and enables learners to interact in spoken communication. L2 learners make
use of listening strategies which help them to understand language input.
They use bottom-up strategies which are text based. The listener relies on the
language in the message, that is, the combination of sounds, words and grammar that creates meaning. Bottom-up strategies include: listening for specific
details; recognizing cognates; and recognizing word-order patterns. However, listening is not just a bottom-up process where learners hear sounds
and need to decode those sounds from the smaller units to large texts but it
is also, as argued by Nunan (2001: 201), a top-down process where learners
reconstruct 'the original meaning of the speaker using incoming sounds as
clues. In this reconstruction process, the listener uses prior knowledge of the
context and situation within which the listening takes place to make sense
of what he or she hears'. Top-down strategies are listener-based where the
listener uses his background knowledge of the topic, and considers the specific situation, the type of text, and the language to interpret the message.
Top-down strategies include: listening for the main idea/concept; predicting;
drawing inferences; summarizing. Learners' comprehension improves and
their confidence increases when they use top-down and bottom-up strategies
simultaneously to construct meaning. L2 learners also tap into metacognitive
strategies to plan, monitor and evaluate their listening. They select the best
listening strategy to use in a particular situation. They monitor their comprehension and the use of the chosen strategy. They evaluate whether or not they
have comprehended the message. Monitoring comprehension helps students
detect inconsistencies and comprehension failures, directing them to the use
of alternate strategies.

   Nunan (2001) and Lee and VanPatten (2003) have all argued that listening
is an active and productive skill. Learners are actively involved in constructing meanings from the messages they hear. For example L2 learners hear a
sentence and need to understand the relevant information to comprehend the
meaning of the message. So for example 'Mr (not Mrs) VanPatten (not Lee)
has sold (not bought) a table (not a cable)'. Learners must be exposed to listening comprehension tasks in which they are actively engaged in processing language to extract the meaning – in this case by processing every single
item; in other cases by extracting the message using other clues.

Therefore, listening comprehension is neither top-down nor bottom-up processing, but an interactive, interpretive process where listeners use both previous knowledge and linguistic knowledge in understanding messages. The use of one process or the other will depend on a series of factors (e.g. language knowledge, topic familiarity, listening purpose). Listening for 'gist' involves primarily top-down processing, whereas listening for specific information, as in a weather broadcast, involves primarily bottom-up processing to fully comprehend the message.

Wolvin and Coakley (1985) have argued that listeners must be active participants during listening comprehension activities. According to Wolvin and Coakley, listeners use a series of mental processes and prior knowledge sources to understand and interpret what they hear. Wolvin and Coakley (1985) argue that listening is a very active skill given that learners are actively engaged in different processes while they are exposed to aural stimuli. Wolvin and Coakley distinguish between three main processes: perceiving; attending; assigning meaning.

As highlighted by Lee and VanPatten (1995: 60), 'perceiving refers to the physiological aspects of listening'. Attending requires 'active concentration by the listener'. Assigning meaning involves 'personal, cultural and linguistic matters interacting in complex ways'. The lesson to learn from these views according to Nunan (2001: 203) is that 'it is important, not only to teach bottom-up processing skills such as the ability to discriminate between minimal parts, but it is also important to help learners use what they already know to understand what they hear'. Research from cognitive psychology has shown that the ability to develop listening skills can't be associated only with the ability to extract meaning from incoming speech. Developing listening skills is instead a process of matching speech with what listeners already know about the topic (Byrnes, 1984). Language instructors must take this into consideration and develop tasks to facilitate L2 learners' activation of prior knowledge and allow them to make the appropriate inferences essential to comprehending the message. Language instructors need to help students organize their thoughts, to activate appropriate background knowledge for understanding and making predictions, to prepare for listening. This significantly reduces the burden of comprehension for the listener.

Other factors that must be taken into consideration when developing a listening task are the difficulty of the listening task and the type of classroom task. In the case of task difficulty we need to take into consideration some of the following factors which might increase or decrease the level of difficulty of a listening comprehension task: speed and level of listening passage;

listeners' role in the listening task; listeners' motivation; content and complexity (e.g. vocabulary, grammar, etc.) of listening passage; non-linguistics items in support of the listening task (e.g. pictures, visual aids). Listeners do not pay attention to everything they hear but they select instead and this is often according to the purpose of the task. Richards (1990) has differentiated between an interactional and a transactional purpose for communication: (a) interactional listening/two-way listening (e.g. talks, conversations) is highly contextualized and involves an interaction component with a speaker; (b) transactional/one-way listening (e.g. news, broadcasts) is more message-oriented and is used primarily to communicate information and requires accurate message comprehension. Knowing the communicative purpose of a text or utterance will help the listener determine what to listen for and, therefore, which processes to activate. As with the advantages of knowing the context, knowing the purpose for listening also greatly reduces the burden of comprehension since listeners know that they need to listen for something very specific, instead of trying to understand every word.

With regard to the types of classroom tasks that might facilitate the development of listening comprehension skills, classroom research suggests that listening tasks should be well structured to allow active participation and interaction from the listener. Task types can be classified in different ways and in the next section we will examine some of the listening comprehension tasks according to the response that L2 learners must produce.

Traditional approaches to listening comprehension tasks encourage passive listening. In traditional practice, L2 learners listen to the teacher or an audio sample and the goal of the task assigned to the listener is to answer a question or fill in the gap. The answer usually highlights the linguistic elements rather than the communicative elements. In a more interactive and communicative approach to listening comprehension tasks, L2 learners are active listeners. They listen to the instructor and each other and the goal of the listening task is to acquire meaning to complete communication. The focus of the listening task is on authentic, contextualized communication. In a more interactive approach to listening comprehension tasks, language instructors should help L2 learners to deal with a variety of situations, types of input, and listening purposes. They should help L2 learners to develop a series of listening strategies (e.g. listening for gist, listening for purpose; see Table 5.1 for a list and examples of key strategies) to be used in different listening situations. Learners must be motivated by a communicative purpose when involved in listening comprehension tasks. In adopting a principled evidence-based approach to the teaching of listening skills, a series of factors needs to be taken into consideration in order to foster the development of listening skills: (a) the role of learners; (b) learners' strategies; (c) type of listening tasks.

Table 5.1 Listening strategies (examples)

Listening for gist: For example: Is the passage about describing living in the city or living in the countryside? Is it a positive or negative view about the current political situation?
Listening for purpose: For example: Is the speaker buying a ticket or making an enquiry? Does John agree or disagree with the death penalty?
Listening for main concepts: For example: Does the speaker like or dislike president Obama? Did John like or dislike the book?
Listening for specific information: How much does the room cost? What time does John meet with Laura?

(a) The role of learners: In everyday life people engage in a variety of situations during which they listen. In developing classroom listening practice we need to take into consideration two types of tasks: collaborative or reciprocal listening; non-collaborative or nonreciprocal listening. Collaborative or reciprocal tasks involve an exchange between two people and negotiation of meaning on both parts (the speaker and the listener). In non-collaborative tasks there is no negotiation of meaning and the listener is only an observant. According to Rost (1990) listeners play an important role in constructing the discourse. Learners are generally engaged in listening tasks that are collaborative and non-collaborative (particularly in the language laboratory).

(b) Learners' strategies: The challenge is to develop listening tasks which will stimulate the development of listening skills while equipping L2 learners with listening strategies. As Littlewood has argued (1981: 67), 'the nature of listening comprehension means that the learner should be encouraged to engage in an active process of listening for meanings, using not only the linguistic cues but also his metalinguistic knowledge'. The listener must be given opportunities to reflect on their learning processes and can be equipped with a range of learning strategies. These strategies, as highlighted by Nunan (2001: 219), would include the ability to listen for specific information, gist or a specific purpose, inferencing and personalizing. L2 learners must be engaged in listening tasks where they make use of bottom-up and top-down strategies. Listeners use metacognitive and cognitive strategies (e.g. to apply a specific technique to a listening task). Cognitive strategies (mental activities used by L2 learners to comprehend and store information in short-term memory) and socio-affective strategies (e.g. to verify understanding) are important processes involved in order to facilitate L2 learners' comprehension. Metacognitive strategies (e.g. assessing the situation, monitoring, self-evaluating, self-assessing) are used to regulate or direct listeners' language learning process. As highlighted by Wenden (1998), when listeners know how to analyse the requirements of a listening task, activate the appropriate listening processes required, make appropriate predictions, monitor their comprehension, and evaluate the success of their approach, they will be more successful in developing listening comprehension skills. Rost (2002) has provided a list of tendencies that successful L2 listeners might display when processing language:

- they tend to predict what they might hear or what might happen;
- they tend to guess what they might hear or what the speakers might have said;
- they tend to focus on key words and select key information;
- they tend to monitor their understanding of the meaning of what they hear;
- they tend to reflect on what they heard and attempt to formulate an opinion, and/or to interact with a speaker, or to personalize the content.

When we develop a listening task we should consider these strategies and incorporate their use directly into our listening tasks.

(c) Type of listening tasks: If we look at listening in the language classroom the two main questions to be asked are: What kind of listening tasks are learners engaged in in the classroom? Do they have the opportunity to develop their skills and strategies? (See Lee and Van Patten, 1995: 66.) Language instructors need to develop listening tasks that integrate listening skills, and to provide opportunities for authentic communicative contexts.

Learners can begin to develop listening skills if instructors take specific steps in developing listening tasks. These are the main principles for designing effective listening tasks:

First of all, language instructors should develop a listening task for a specific communicative purpose (form or response such as doing, answering...)

using motivating topics which relate to learners' needs and interests. L2 learners must be motivated by a communicative purpose and need to extract meaning from a listening text. In order to do that, they need to figure out the purpose for listening. Instructors need to design a listening task which will activate learners' background knowledge about the specific topic in order to predict or anticipate the content of the listening task and identify appropriate listening strategies in order to complete the task. In listening for a specific purpose, learners need only to attend to the parts of the listening input that are relevant to the identified purpose.

This selectivity helps learners to focus on specific items in the input and reduces the amount of information they have to hold in short-term memory in order to recognize it.

Second, language instructors need to develop contextualized tasks. Contextualized listening tasks provide the listener with an idea of the type of information to expect and what to do with it before the actual listening. The content of these tasks will vary depending on the L2 learner's proficiency level. At beginning level, learners might be asked to locate places on a map. At an intermediate level, they could reconstruct a story to tell to the rest of the class. The listening task should be based on authentic text, both monologues and dialogues.

Third, language instructors need to define the task's instructional goal and type of response. L2 learners must know what they are listening for and why. Each task should have as its goal the improvement of one or more specific listening skills. Language instructors should identify the goal(s) of a listening comprehension task to direct L2 learners in selecting appropriate listening strategies (e.g. recognizing specific aspects of the message, such as sounds, words, morphological distinctions; determining the topic about a message; comprehending main ideas).

Fourth, language instructors should take into consideration the level of difficulty of the listening text. In achieving this, they need to consider the following factors: how the information is presented; how familiar learners are with the topic; whether the listening task offers visual support (e.g. maps, diagrams, pictures) to contextualize the listening input and provide clues to meaning.

Fifth, language instructors should make use of pre-listening tasks to prepare students for what they are going to hear or view. Pre-listening tasks would motivate and activate learners' knowledge and interest. These tasks assess learners' background knowledge, and provide them with the background knowledge necessary for their comprehension, e.g. reviewing relevant vocabulary or grammatical structures before listening to a passage; reading something relevant to the listening task; predicting the content of the listening text; think-pair-share (pair technique to guess content); brainstorming. This will also allow learners to play an active role in their learning. Pre-listening tasks help students make decisions about what to listen for and, subsequently, to focus attention on meaning while listening. Language instructors need to raise learners' consciousness/knowledge of the relevant topic. They also need to establish a listening purpose so that L2 learners know the specific information they need to listen for, and to enable them to make predictions by anticipating what they might hear.

Sixth, language instructors should encourage the development of listening strategies by exposing L2 learners to different ways of processing information such as bottom-up tasks (e.g. word-sentence recognition, listening for different morphological endings), top-down tasks (identifying the topic, understanding the meaning of a sentence), and interactive tasks (e.g. listening to a list and categorizing the words, following directions).

Learners must be exposed to a variety of tasks in order to develop listening strategies such as looking for key words, looking for non-verbal cues to meaning, associating information with one's existing background knowledge (activating schemata), guessing meanings, listening for the general gist, seeking clarification. Littelewood (1981: 68) has provided a typology of listening tasks based on the active nature of listening comprehension and the understanding that L2 learners must listen to a text for a specific purpose. He has discussed and identified different types of listening comprehension tasks that will help learners to develop their listening skills and improve their listening strategies. He has grouped the tasks according to the response learners must produce. The two main categories are:

- listening tasks where learners perform physical tasks;
- listening tasks where learners transfer information.

In the case of performing physical tasks L2 learners are asked to process specific information in the message they hear. Learners can be asked to focus their attention on specific features by scanning the aural text for specific information. They are encouraged to listen and look for specific meanings. In the example below (see Activity 5.1) the instructor can do the actions while she/he is speaking and learners need to perform these actions as instructed.

You are going to hear the teacher of a keep-fit exercise class giving instructions to participants while they do the warm-up exercises.

Right, everybody. Stand up straight. Now bend forward and down to touch your toes—and up—and down—and up. Arms by your sides. Raise your right knee as high as you can. Hold your leg with both hands and pull your knee back against your body. Keep your backs straight. Now lower your leg and do the same with your right knee—up—pull towards you—and raise your arms to shoulder level. Squeeze your fists tightly in front of your chest. Now push your elbows back—keep your head up! And relax... Feet together, and put your hands on your hips. Now bend your knees and stretch your arms out to the sides at shoulder height, palms up. Rotate your arms in small circles—That's right—and now the other way. Now stand with your hands clasped behind your neck and your legs apart. Bend over to the left, slowly, but as far as you can. And slowly up. And down to the right. And up. OK—if we are all warmed up now, let's begin!

Activity 5.1 Task A (from Zhang, 2000: 102–103)

In the case of listening tasks where learners transfer information, learners not only have to extract some meaningful information from the text but also need to transfer (e.g. filling in a table, completing a chart) some specific information in order to complete the task. In contrast to previous examples, activities in this category do not demand that students respond physically to what they hear. In addition, students are asked to put pictures in order or transfer what they hear in the form of a table, chart or diagram. Learners are still required to look for specific types of meaning in tasks such as identification and selection, sequencing tasks and location tasks.

Alternatively L2 learners hear a description or a conversation and decide, from the selection offered, which picture is the right one. Learners may have also several pictures and listen to one short description or dialogue, and then decide the dialogue or description that matches each picture. In the case of sequencing tasks, learners are asked to identify successive pictures that are described or mentioned, in order to place them in their correct sequence. To make this kind of exercise more complicated, we may increase the number and the similarity of pictures to increase the language complexity and raise the delivery speed to a higher level of difficulty. In locating tasks, learners are required to place items not into a sequence, but into their appropriate location. Alternatively they may listen to a description and trace the route being described. Again the nature of the language input and the language difficulty can vary.

Seventh, language instructors need to provide listeners with the opportunity to monitor their comprehension and make decisions about strategy used during a listening task. Learners need to evaluate continually what they comprehend, and check consistency with their predictions and interpretation of the passage. Learners also need to evaluate the results of decisions made during a listening task. Language instructors can facilitate self-evaluation by asking learners to assess the effectiveness of the particular strategies learners have used (e.g. class or group discussions). In order to help L2 learners consciously focus on planning, monitoring and evaluation before and after the completion of listening tasks, language instructors should use performance checklists (see, for example, Vandergrift, 2002).

In Activity 5.2 we present a task in which we have put the main principles presented in this chapter into practice. The design of a listening comprehension task is influenced by factors such as time frame, learners' interests and abilities. The listening task provided here is adopted from Rost and Fuchs (2002). The text is about a sports celebrity called Lance Armstrong. The text is intended for an intermediate level class. A pre-listening task stage is developed to enable students to activate what they already know, predict information and/or to deal with problematic vocabulary and structures. During the listening stage, language instructors can develop tasks in which L2 learners are asked to match short phrases with a list of dates, and/or identify specific words in the passage. In the post-listening task stage learners are asked to articulate their ideas and clarify meanings. Learners are given the opportunity to 'personalize' their understanding of the passage and monitor their own progress.

Listening Text

In the current TV spotlight is Lance Armstrong, 'The Golden Boy of Cycling'. Lance Armstrong was born on 18 September 1971 in a small Texas town. From early on, it was clear that he was a natural athlete. In 1984, at age 13, Lance won a national triathlon, excelling at running, swimming and cycling. By 1987, while he was still in high school, Lance had turned professional. He decided to focus exclusively on cycling, saying, 'I was born to race bikes.' Between 1988 and 1996, Armstrong won numerous international races. In January 1996 he was the top-ranked cyclist in the world. Then, during a race in October of that year, Armstrong fell off his bike in excruciating pain. They discovered that he had cancer, which had spread to his lungs and brain. Given only a 50 per cent chance of survival, in 1997 Armstrong underwent difficult cancer treatment. Amazingly, he not only survived, he returned to competition, winning several major races in 1998. Since that time, Armstrong has gone on to win many more races, including the Tour de France in 1999, 2000, and 2001. Lance says that cancer was an unexpected gift. 'I used to ride my bike to make a living. Now I just want to live so that I can ride.'

Pre-listening task stage

a)   Many great athletes are known not only for their victories on the playing field but also for their personal triumphs away from their sport. World champion cyclist Lance Armstrong is one such person.
What do you know about him? Work with a partner. List what you know about him.

b)   Here are some expressions from the passage you will hear. Listen to the teacher say them. Are you familiar with these expressions?

- It was clear that...
- He excelled at...
- They discovered that...
- Amazingly, he...
- It was an unexpected gift.
- I used to..., but now I...

While-listening task stage

a) Listen to this 'TV Minute', spotlighting Lance Armstrong, 'The Golden Boy of Cycling'. Listen for dates and key events in his life. As you listen, look at the time-line below. Listen for one event for each date on the time-line. Write a short phrase for each event.

1971 1984 1986 1988–1996 1996 1997 1999 2000 2001

b) Read these sentences. Some of these are in the passage. Listen again. Which of these phrases are in the passage? Check them.
- From the time he was a child, it was clear that he was a natural-born athlete.
- While he was still in high school, Lance was turning professional.
- He decided to focus primarily on cycling.
- By January 1996 he was the top-ranked cyclist in the country.
- Armstrong had fallen off his bike in excruciating pain.
- It had been discovered that he had cancer.
- Since that time, Armstrong has been able to win many more races.
- Armstrong has said that cancer was an unnecessary gift.

Post-listening task stage

a) Work with a partner. Compare your time-lines. Give extra information about each event.

b) Do you have any questions about the passage? Are there any new vocabulary words? Ask your teacher now. Use these phrases:
- What does '…' mean?
- I heard a phrase that sounded like '…' I'm not familiar with that.
- I couldn't catch the part after '…'

c) Listen to the passage one last time. In your own words, what is the theme of this 'TV Minute'? What feeling do you get when you listen to the passage? Do you know anyone like Lance Armstrong?

d) Evaluate this passage and the tasks.

Passage:
not very	a little	very interesting
☐	☐	☐

How difficult was this passage and the tasks for you?
not so difficult	a little difficult	very difficult
☐	☐	☐

Which task was most useful for you?
Did your partner help you understand the passage better? How?
Would you change any of the tasks? How?

Activity 5.2 Listening task

Conclusion

In developing effective listening comprehension tasks, instructors must not give learners irrelevant detailed comprehension questions and engage in tasks where learners listen and repeat everything. Instead, language instructors should set the context through interactions and stimulate motivation. They should make the listening tasks authentic and central to the listening lesson and involve students in the listening through negotiation of meaning. Learners should be guided through the process of listening in order to provide the necessary knowledge by which they can successfully complete a listening task. A listening comprehension task must be designed for a purpose, have a clear set of procedures and a tangible outcome, and must be monitored and evaluated by the teacher, who can provide some form of feedback and evaluation on performance.

Based on these assumptions, a three-stage approach is proposed:

- In the pre-listening stage, language instructors should set the context, create motivation and activate learners' prior knowledge through cooperative learning tasks (e.g. brainstorming, think-pair-share). Effective listening tasks involve learners predicting ideas and pre-structuring relevant information in the text. Pre-listening tasks include vocabulary learning and/or identifying key ideas contained in the upcoming input.
- In the while-listening stage, learners are required to listen for main ideas to establish the context and transfer information. Learners are exposed to bottom-up tasks (e.g. word-sentence recognition, listening for different morphological endings), top-down tasks (identifying the topic, understanding meaning of sentences) and interactive tasks (e.g. listening to a list and categorizing the words, following directions). Main listening tasks at this stage include guided note taking, completion of a picture or schematic diagram or table.
- The post-listening stage helps learners to examine the functional language and infer the meaning of vocabulary (e.g. guess the meaning of unknown vocabulary, analyse the success of communication in the script, brainstorm alternative ways of expression). In the final stage, language learners are given post-listening tasks which involve reading, writing, speaking, and interaction activities.

Suggested Reading

Field, J. (2008). *Listening in the Language Classroom.* Cambridge: Cambridge University Press.

This book challenges the traditional approach to the teaching of listening skills. The book proposes a radical and psychological alternative to the teaching of listening skills.

Rost, M. (1990). *Listening in Language Learning.* London: Longman.

This volume examines the role of listening in language learning. It provides an analysis of how listening development can be incorporated effectively in second language teaching.

Rost, M. (2002). *Teaching and Researching Listening: Applied Linguistics in Action.* London: Longman.

This book provides an up-to date summary of teaching and research in listening skills.

6 Key Issues in the Teaching of Reading

Chapter Preview

In this chapter, the role of reading comprehension in second language learning and teaching will be discussed.

An interactive and communicative approach to teaching reading skills will be proposed.

At the end of the chapter, general guidelines as to how to develop effective tasks that help L2 learners improve their reading and comprehension skills will be offered.

Introduction

In this chapter an approach to reading comprehension is given, suggesting that L2 learners can process and understand a written text even though there are vocabulary items and structures learners have never seen before. Reading to extract specific information can be satisfactorily performed even though learners do not understand the whole text. An interactive approach to reading will be examined in this chapter. This approach is centred on the idea that L2 learners need to learn reading skills that extract specific information and not to translate texts. It is vital to train learners to develop the ability to understand written passages without understanding every single word.

Learners are often asked to read slowly and worry about the meaning of each particular word. Traditionally, the purpose of learning to read in a language has been to have access to the literature written in that language and develop the ability to translate literary texts. This approach assumes that students learn to read a language by studying its vocabulary, grammar and sentence structure. The reading of authentic materials is totally absent in this practice.

In the approach to reading comprehension presented in this chapter, developing reading skills is seen as developing the ability to read in another language. L2 learners read texts in another language for a specific purpose. They read in order to gain specific information. The purpose(s) for reading must guide the reader's selection of texts. In addition to that, authentic material should be used by language instructors. When the goal of instruction is communicative competence, everyday materials such as train schedules, newspaper articles, and travel and touristic brochures become appropriate classroom materials. The approach is based on the understanding that the ability to read and comprehend a text is based not only on the reader's linguistic knowledge, but also on general knowledge of the world and the learner's ability to activate that knowledge during reading.

Key Aspects

Reading is considered an interactive process between the reader and the text and results in comprehension. The text presents letters, words, sentences and paragraphs that encode meaning. The reader uses knowledge, skills and strategies to determine what that meaning is. Readers need to develop the ability to recognize the elements of the writing system (e.g. word recognition, grammatical features); they need to develop knowledge of discourse and how different parts of the text connect with each other; they need to develop a knowledge about different types of texts; and the need to be able to use top-down and bottom-up strategies. Developing reading comprehension skills can be defined as the reader's ability to use and apply appropriate skills and strategies in order to successfully comprehend a written text.

Key Developments

Research on the development of reading comprehension has provided important insights in various areas. Research findings on developing learners' ability to process language sounds have revealed that it is an important skill and it is highly correlated with reading ability. Research on word recognition has indicated that recognizing a word is a necessary component in comprehending a text. However, it is not sufficient to develop fluent reading skills. Readers must construct meaning from the words he/she can recognize. Language instructors should provide guided practice in reading in order to increase learners' fluency. Good readers must develop good vocabulary knowledge. Language instructors must provide multiple exposure to vocabulary.

Developing learners' comprehension is the process of constructing meaning from a text. It involves word knowledge (vocabulary) as well as thinking and reasoning. This process involves making use of learners' prior knowledge. It involves drawing from internal strategies to process words and expressions in the input that learners hear. Likewise in the development of listening skills, reading skills are affected by two processing strategies: bottom-up and top-down. Bottom-up strategies are used by L2 learners to gradually decode the linguistics information (e.g. orthographic knowledge, lexical and syntactic knowledge) in a written text: from the small to large units. Readers process letters and characters, and analyse and interpret the meaning of words and sentences. Top-down strategies involve processing beyond the analysis of linguistics information (e.g. knowledge of text structure, prior knowledge such as topic familiarity, cultural awareness). The so-called Schema theory (Lee and VanPatten, 1995, 2003) suggests that, as learners, our knowledge impacts on how we process and understand new incoming information. As argued by Nunan (2001: 257), 'the basic principle behind schema theory is that texts themselves, whether spoken or written, do not carry meaning; rather they provide signposts, or clues to be utilized by listeners or readers in reconstructing the original meaning of speakers or writers'.

Research in reading has had the following pedagogical implications for developing reading skills:

- pre-reading activities are very effective in improving schema activation and use of reading strategies;
- reading should be done for a real-life specific purpose;
- learners should read extensively;
- learners should be encouraged to integrate information in the text with existing knowledge;
- learners should be motivated and should engage in reading tasks with a specific purpose;
- learners should be engaged in tasks stimulating different skills (e.g. perceptual processing, phonemic processing).

L2 learners tend not to transfer the strategies they use when reading in their native language to reading into another language. When reading a text from another language they exclusively rely on their linguistic knowledge (a bottom-up strategy). One challenge for the language instructor is to help L2 learners not to rely on this bottom-up strategy but use top-down strategies as they do in their native language. Some of these strategies can help L2 learners to read effectively in the language they are learning. Previewing a text might help learners to develop a general understanding of the content of a passage.

Using readers' pre-existing knowledge might help in making predictions about content, discourse structure, vocabulary and main concepts in a text. Skimming and scanning might help learners to understand the main ideas in the text and confirm or question predictions. Guessing from context might help learners to decode the meanings of unknown words rather than translating word by word. Paraphrasing might help learners to summarize the main ideas and concepts in a text using their own words.

Language instructors can help learners to use these reading strategies in several ways. They can take learners through the processes of previewing, predicting, skimming and scanning, and paraphrasing. They should allow enough time in the classroom for group previewing and predicting activities in preparation for a reading comprehension task. They should develop tasks that encourage learners to guess meaning from context. When language learners are able to use reading strategies, they will be able to effectively develop their ability to read into another language.

There are issues related to topic interest, language difficulty and topic familiarity, addressed by scholars in second language acquisition research (see Brantmeier, 2009), which account for a significant variation in comprehension. Learners would find it difficult to process complex language and unfamiliar topics. It is desirable that teachers select a text according to the learner's familiarity with the topic.

An effective way to teach learners' reading abilities is for language instructors to help them develop reading strategies that they can use in different reading tasks. Reading is a key part of language instruction as it supports learning in multiple ways. When L2 learners are exposed to a variety of materials to read, they have many opportunities to process vocabulary, grammar and sentence structure in authentic contexts. Also learners develop a better picture of how these elements of the language work together to convey meaning. Reading for content information in the language classroom provides learners with both authentic reading material and an authentic purpose for reading. When reading to learn, students need to follow four basic steps:

1. Figure out the purpose for reading. Activate background knowledge of the topic in order to predict or anticipate content and identify appropriate reading strategies.

2. Attend to the parts of the text that are relevant to the identified purpose and ignore the rest. This selectivity enables students to focus on specific items in the input and reduces the amount of information they have to hold in short-term memory.

3. Select strategies that are appropriate to the reading task and use them flexibly and interactively. Students' comprehension improves and their confidence increases when they use top-down and bottom-up skills simultaneously to construct meaning.

4. Check comprehension while reading and when the reading task is completed. Monitoring comprehension helps students detect inconsistencies and comprehension failures, helping them learn to use alternate strategies.

The pedagogical implication of the Schema theory is the understanding that reading is an interactive process between readers and texts. Readers must associate elements in a text with their pre-reading knowledge (Rumelhart, 1980).

Reading activities in traditional textbooks consists mainly of two types: translation tasks (read a passage and translate into Japanese); answer questions from a text (a typical task/exercise is: Read the dialogue/text and answer the following questions).

Reading should be viewed, as claimed by Lee and Van Patten (1995: 189), as 'reading in another language rather than as an exercise in translation'. The fact that language learners do not necessarily have the verbal virtuosity of a native reader means instructors need to use some strategies to help them. The framework presented here takes into consideration the need to guide learners in their comprehension of a text. In adopting a principled evidence-based approach to the teaching of reading skills, a series of measures need to be taken in order to foster the development of oral skills. Instructors should develop reading activities following a five-stage approach: pre-reading stage; reading stage; text-interaction stage; post-reading stage; personalization stage. When designing a reading task, language instructors must keep in mind that we cannot expect learners to process all the information in a text.

The purpose of the reading comprehension tasks presented in Figure 6.1 is to bridge the gap between the reader and the information contained in the text.

Pre-reading tasks must be included to activate learners' existing knowledge. In order to prepare the learners and activate their knowledge relevant to a particular reading text, many techniques are available. Some of these have been highlighted by Lee and VanPatten (1995: 199–204):

- Brainstorming as a whole-class exercise or in pairs. This can take place before reading the text and should help to bridge the gap between the reader and a text.
- Titles, subtitle, headings, divisions within the text, and illustrations can be exploited as a means to activate learners' background knowledge and/or to predict content.
- Scanning for specific information can be used in the case of a text that does not need extensive preparation. We could ask learners to scan the text for specific information, to skim to find the theme or main idea and to elicit information activating appropriate prior knowledge.

In Activity 6.1 (pre-reading stage), L2 learners are asked to read the title of the text and based on that to write down some of the issues they expect to find in the text. Before this pre-reading task, learners are asked to work in pairs and talk about some of the issues related to the main topic of the reading text. Both tasks are designed to activate readers' knowledge that will be needed to be used to understand the information in the text. This is an attempt to bridge the gap between the readers and the text. Pre-reading tasks serve the purpose of mainly preparing learners for the reading task. However, during pre-reading, language instructors have the opportunity to assess learners' background knowledge of the topic and linguistic content of the text, to provide learners with the background knowledge necessary for the comprehension of the text, to activate their existing knowledge, and to clarify key issues which may be necessary to comprehend the passage.

During the reading stage L2 learners are asked to scan the text for specific information. Initially, readers should process the text to understand the general meaning. In the example in Activity 6.1 learners are asked to quickly scan the text to establish whether or not they have guessed the content of the text during pre-reading activities.

In the text-interaction stage L2 learners explore fully the content of a text. We should guide learners through this process so as to avoid learners reading word for word. Language instructors must make sure that learners understand what the purpose of reading is. Learners must get the main ideas, obtain specific information, and gradually understand most of the message. Recognizing the purpose of reading will help students to select appropriate reading strategies. This stage consists of a combination of two types of tasks (Lee and VanPatten, 1995: 204):

- management strategies in which we suggest ways to divide a text into small parts;
- comprehension checks implemented during the guided interaction phase so that readers are continuously monitored.

In the text-interaction tasks, L2 learners must check their comprehension as they read. In Activity 6.1, readers are asked to interact with the text by exploring a part or section of the passage.

In the post-reading stage learners are given a series of tasks in which they organize the information in the text (see Lee and VanPatten, 1995: 207). The post-reading tasks in Activity 6.1 are designed to check and verify comprehension. The purpose of these tasks is to encourage readers to learn from what they have read.

In the personalization stage (see Activity 6.1) learners are encouraged to exploit the communicative function of the reading text through the use of the text to accomplish a specific task (e.g. solve a problem, create a poster, apply main concepts to another context, relate key issues to a different context).

Conclusion

Developing reading comprehension skills involves the interaction of a variety of knowledge sources. An interactive model for the comprehension of written language has been proposed. This model envisages that L2 learners make a positive contribution to their learning. The proposed framework for developing reading comprehension tasks comprises different stages. Based on the principles highlighted in this chapter, instructors should be supplied with the following guidelines for the development of effective reading comprehension tasks:

- Reading comprehension tasks should be constructed around a purpose that has significance for learners. This will stimulate their motivation and interest.
- Reading comprehension tasks should be developed by language instructors for a specific purpose and language instructors should make sure that L2 learners understand what the purpose of reading is. A task can have more than one instructional purpose (e.g. practising a specific grammatical structure, introducing new vocabulary, familiarizing learners with a particular topic).
- Reading comprehension tasks should have a defined goal and develop tasks for learners to deliver appropriate responses.

Pre-reading stage

a)   Discuss with your partner the following issues around 'smoking'
-    What do you think of 'smoking'?
-    What are the risks?
-    What would you do to resolve the problem?

b) Read the title of the text and write a couple of ideas/concepts you are predicting to find in the main text.
World No Tobacco Day
-
-

Reading stage

c) Read the text quickly to find out whether you have correctly guessed the main concepts.

1.   Smoking kills six million people every year around the world, and more than half a million non-smokers are affected from second-hand smoke. According to the World Health Organization (WHO), tobacco use is the leading cause of preventable death. In fact, tobacco kills more people every year than alcohol, AIDS, car accidents, illegal drugs, murders and suicides combined. Unless more people quit smoking, this deadly habit could kill up to one billion people in the 21st century.

2.   The World No Tobacco Day (WNTD) is observed worldwide every year on May 31st to help smokers abstain from consuming tobacco for at least 24 hours; smokers are also encouraged to give up the habit for life. WNTD was started in 1987, when the World Health Assembly (WHA) of the WHO passed a resolution which formed the initiative. The primary aim of WNTD is to educate people about the deadly nature of tobacco. Each year on this day WHO chooses a theme that carries a message to quit smoking and raise awareness of the dangers of smoking. This year WHO has taken a new direction that stresses the legal side of tobacco prevention, as opposed to the typical 'awareness' theme. WHO is per-suading more countries to sign a global treaty to ensure public protec-tion from smoking. The treaty, 'The WHO Framework Convention on Tobacco Control' (FCTC) is known as the world's primary tobacco ces-sation instrument, and is the focus for the theme this year. The treaty was drafted six years ago and 172 countries have signed it, though 20 percent have done nothing to implement its recommendations. In addition, major countries such as the U.S. and Indonesia have not even signed it.

3. In the U.S. tobacco abuse is responsible for 440,000 deaths annually. Eighty percent of adult smokers begin smoking before age 18. Adolescents who smoke are more likely to drink heavily and more likely to use illicit drugs than their non-smoking counterparts. In addition, adolescents who smoke are more likely to have panic disorders and other anxiety disorders. In Indonesia there are 21 million child smokers. There is essentially nothing to stop companies promoting cigarettes to youth. In countries such as Brazil and Nigeria tobacco companies sponsor party nights to attract new young users. In Russia, women are persuaded to smoke by selling cigarettes branded by the fashion giant Yves Saint Laurent.

4. For countries that have signed the treaty, the WHO FCTC places certain requests including obligations to:

    – Protect public health policies from commercial and other interests of the tobacco industry
    – Protect people from exposure to tobacco smoke
    – Warn people about the dangers of tobacco
    – Regulate the packaging and labelling of tobacco products
    – Offer people help to end their addiction to tobacco
    – Ban cigarette sale to and by minors
    – Support economically viable alternatives to tobacco growing.

    The WNTD campaign will focus on fully implementing the treaty to protect present and future generations from the consequences of tobacco consumption and exposure. If more people give up smoking this will be a major victory for health services worldwide. It will help prevent millions of unnecessary deaths and save a huge amount in health care costs. Not to mention, the next generation will be healthier.
    From Natural News http://www.naturalnews.com/032578_tobacco_smoking.html#ixzz1WVfqGt8y

Text-interaction stage

d) Read the four sections of the text and reflect on its content. For each section write a short paragraph summarizing the main meaning.

-
-
-
-

e) Based on what you have read indicate whether these statements are true or false.

True / False
1. Alcohol kills fewer people than drugs and AIDS.
2. In the US most people begin smoking at 18.
3. The majority of children's deaths is in Brazil.
4. WNTD was created in the late eighties.
5. Over one hundred and seventy countries have signed the new treaty.

f) Find the synonyms of the following words in the text.

1. avoidable

2. illicit

3. convince

4. decision

5. illness

Post-reading stage

g) Step 1: Work with your partner and identify four possible solutions to the problem of 'smoking'.
-
-
-
-

Step 2: Working with the other groups in class prepare a poster against 'smoking'.

Personalization stage

h) Working in groups, prepare an interview/questionnaire on the main issues concerned with smoking.
Questions

Activity 6.1 Interactive reading task

- Use pre-reading tasks to prepare students for reading and activate their background knowledge.
- Use text-interaction reading tasks to gradually bridge the gap between the text and the reader.
- Use post-reading tasks to check and verify comprehension.
- Use personalization tasks to encourage learners to exploit the communicative function of the reading text.

Suggested Reading

Anderson, N. (1999). *Exploring Second Language Reading: Issues and Strategies.* Boston, MA: Heinle and Heinle.

This volume explores the different elements of reading instruction. The approach to reading comprehension proposed is called ACTIVE. ACTIVE consists of the first letters of six of the eight elements of this approach: activate prior knowledge; cultivate vocabulary; teach for comprehension; increase reading rate; verify reading strategies; evaluate progress. The last two elements are: consider the role of motivation and select appropriate materials.

Bernhardt, E. (1991). *Reading Development in a Second Language.* Norwood, NJ: Ablex.

This book aims at providing an account of what is known about the acquisition of reading abilities in second language acquisition. The author supports a principled and research-evidence approach to the development of reading skills.

Brantmeier, C. (ed.) 2009. *Crossing Languages and Research Methods: Analyses of Adult Foreign Language Reading.* Greenwich, CT: Information Age Publishing.

This book provides important research findings that will assist foreign language teachers in developing effective reading comprehension tasks.

7 Key Issues in the Teaching of Writing

Chapter Preview

In this chapter, a process-oriented approach to writing will be examined. This approach engages the writer in the creation of a text rather than just focusing on the final product.

A theory of writing which is at the basis of a process-oriented approach to developing writing skills in the language classroom will be presented.

Finally, general guidelines as to how to develop effective written tasks that will help learners improve their written skills in a second language will be offered.

Introduction

One of the major developments in second language pedagogy has been the shift from product-oriented approaches to process-oriented approaches in the teaching of language writing skills. Process-oriented approaches focus on the creation of a text rather than concentrating only on the final product. In this chapter, the role of language writing in second language teaching from a communicative perspective is examined. Writing, like any other aspects of second language development, is about communication. In real life we write emails, notes, letters, grocery lists, reports, essays, etc. All these different tasks have a communicative purpose and a specific audience.

In this chapter, a more communicative approach to the development of writing skills is proposed. This approach takes into consideration a cognitive-process theory of writing. Writing is a somewhat neglected skill in second language teaching, and, very often, writing tasks set up by language instructors might not be motivating for language learners and not properly incorporated into a language lesson. In order to develop more effective tasks for developing writing skills, language instructors must clarify the communicative purpose of a written task and the target audience. Language instructors must integrate writing with other language skills and use more meaningful, realistic and relevant writing tasks based on learners' needs. In the next paragraphs the most famous cognitive-process theory of writing put forward by Flower and Hayes (1981) will be presented and its pedagogical implications highlighted.

Key Aspects

The development of writing skills will help L2 learners to gain independence, fluency and creativity in language writing. In developing writing skills, learners improve the way they put their thoughts into words in a meaningful and accurate way, and also improve their mental interaction with the message they want to convey.

Before starting to write, learners must define the rhetorical problem (i.e. why do I write, the purpose of the text to be written, the recipient of the written text, the topic, as well as the learner's knowledge about the topic). Furthermore, the learner should plan the writing, which includes several sub-processes such as planning, generating ideas, organizing ideas and setting goals. This brief description of the processes involved in writing tells us how dynamic and complex writing is, regardless of whether the learner writes in his/her mother tongue or other languages.

In this chapter the development of written tasks as part of a communication process is discussed. Current approaches to teaching writing focus on the actual writing process as supposed to focusing exclusively on the writing product. We often refer to these types of communicative tasks as 'composing tasks' as opposed to 'writing tasks' which involves, in a more generic way, any type of production activities. When we write a grocery list we accomplish an act of communication (Lee and Van Patten, 1995: 215).

Key Developments

In the last twenty years we have witnessed two main developments in the study of cognitive processes involved in writing. The first is the fact that writing is not simply a matter of translating preconceived ideas into text, but also involves creating content and tailoring this content taking into account the reader's needs. The second is that writing involves a complex interaction between a wide range of different processes and learners adopt specific strategies to cope with the task of writing.

As highlighted by Lee and VanPatten (1995: 216), Flower and Hayes (1981) propose a cognitive-processing second language instruction model which emphasizes learners' mental processes. According to this theory, the cognitive process in writing involves a series of sub-processes. Writing is a process where learners explore, consolidate and develop rhetorical objectives. According to Flower and Hayes (1981) the act of writing involves three major elements:

- the task environment which includes things external to the writer such as the rhetorical problem and the text itself;
- the writer's long-term memory which includes the knowledge of the topic, the audience, and various writing plans;
- the writing process which involves three basic processes: planning, which include generating ideas, organization and goal setting as components; translating plans into text; and reviewing, which include reading and editing as components.

The rhetorical problem includes the rhetorical situation, the audience and the writer's goals. It is crucial that learners do not reduce these issues to just a simple task, i.e. 'write a paper in English'. The text itself is also competing with the knowledge in the writer's long-term memory and the writer's plans for dealing with the rhetorical problem.

This model is different from the traditional product-based model of writing which is a linear process of planning, writing and editing. The three processes in the cognitive-process model (planning, translating and revising) can, in principle, occur at any moment during writing. However, the monitor in Hayes and Flower's model plays a key role in controlling the writing process, deciding when enough content has been generated and whether or not revision is necessary. The planning process contains three sub-processes: generating ideas which includes retrieving information from long-term memory; organizing which includes allowing the writer to identify categories; searching for ideas; reaching a specific audience; setting a goal.

The translating process includes the ability to put ideas into words. It requires the writer to juggle all the various demands of the new language.

The reviewing process depends on two sub-processes: evaluating and revising. It may be a conscious process when the writer chooses to reread for new ideas or to evaluate and revise the physical text. It may be an unconscious action triggered by an evaluation of the text or planning.

In current language textbooks written activities focus on production of grammatical and lexical structures. The task in Activity 7.1 is a typical

Write a story/composition about how young people can spend their winter vacation in Macedonia using some of the elements in the three columns as a guide.

happy	hotel	visit
soon	House	coming
always	Lake	booked
hardly	You	mountaineers
nice	mountain	travel
together	culture	found
difficult	holiday	sport

Activity 7.1 Traditional writing task

example of traditional writing practices and it is often used in current language textbooks. L2 learners are provided with a list of words some of which they must use to write a short paragraph. It can be argued that in this task the rhetorical problem for learners is reduced to producing a text using grammatical and lexical items. The focus of the task is to produce a text that contains particular lexical and grammatical items.

Writing processes are minimal as the content is not as important as the use of the specific items. Planning will consist of constructing and ordering individual sentences. Reviewing will focus on which items in the list were used.

Traditional approaches to the teaching of L2 writing have focused on linguistic rules and vocabulary. Process-oriented approaches have shifted the focus on the audience and the purpose of writing. Communicative Language Teaching and Task-based Instruction engage L2 learners in authentic and interactive writing activities. Lee and VanPatten (1995: 222) proposed an interactive approach to writing practices called 'composing-oriented activities'. This approach, based on the model presented by Flower and Hayes, aims at improving L2 learners' writing skills. The main goal of this approach is to develop tasks which would help learners with the conceptual definition of the rhetorical problem and involve higher processes of planning and reviewing. Their model consists of two main phases:

- Pre-writing activities in which L2 learners are given different options so that they can make choices and decide in which direction to develop their composition;

- Writing stage that begins immediately after the previous phase and during which L2 learners become aware of the elements of good writing.

The following is a sample of the various steps (from Lee and Van Patten, 1995: 222–23) used in developing a composing activity from the pre-writing phase to the writing phase:

Step 1 (Generating content): Instructor assigns one topic to students in groups.
Step 2 (Defining audience and content): Each group has an amount of time to make a list of ideas related to that topic.
Step 3 (Planning and organizing): Each group should copy the lists from the other groups to be used later in writing.
Step 4 (Composing): Take your outline and list of ideas and write your composition.

Learners should write a draft of the work and let it sit sometime. They should ask themselves two questions: Are these still the ideas I want to include? Does the order in which the ideas are presented help get my message across? If the answer is no, they should rewrite the composition.

Activity 7.2 illustrates the approach proposed by Lee and VanPatten and provides a task which engages learners and improves their writing. The task in Activity 7.2, adapted from Lee and VanPatten (1995: 222–23), allows L2 learners to become aware of the various elements of good writing. In this task, learners have to take into consideration the rhetorical problem; they need to plan well and make appropriate decisions about the ideas they generate and how to organize them; finally they need to put ideas on paper and then review them. The difference between the two written tasks (Activities 7.1 and 7.2) lies not only in the quality of the text produced, but also in the manner and/or the process through which the text was generated.

First of all, this approach will help the writer to explore and then to consolidate ideas. Exploration often occurs at the beginning of the process. Consolidation produces a more complex idea by drawing inferences and creating concepts. Secondly, the writer starts with high-level goals and then fleshes out the sub-goals. As the goals become more concrete, the writer finds the connection between ideas and intentions for the actual text. Finally, the writer will have the opportunity to write and review their writing.

Generating content

Step 1. To each group of three to four students, the teacher assigns one of the two topics:

Winter holidays for young people in Macedonia 20 years ago
Winter holidays for young people in Macedonia today

Each group will have ten minutes to write as many ideas as possible related to the topic, and for each element of the following:

1. natural beauties of Macedonia
2. sports centres and resorts
3. recreational and sport habits of young people
4. economic opportunities for citizens
5. entertainment.

Step 2. Once all the groups have drawn up lists of ideas, each group will present them to the class, and then the teacher will write a common list on the board and ask them whether they have any other ideas to add.

Step. 3 Each student will copy the common list so that later s/he can use it to compose the essay. When generating the ideas, the teacher can supply additional materials (books, tourist guides, internet, etc.) to give additional input of formal written language and additional knowledge that students may not possess.

Define audience and purpose

Step 1. Taking into account the ideas that students have generated in the previous activity, students should consider the readers of the text/ composition. The teacher can suggest they choose any of the following:

– friends from abroad you have met during the summer holiday
– pen-friends
– former friends or neighbours of another ethnic group who have moved to another country and are coming to visit after many years
– other suggestions _____.

Step 2. Each student should choose one of the two topics and form groups of three students working on the same topic together and write the characteristics of the selected reader (audience). Then, each group will present the characteristics to the whole class, while students are encouraged to help their peers by adding features they may not have thought of.

Planning and organizing

Step 1. Once the audience, that is the readers, is defined the teacher encourages them to think what they would say. The working groups from the previous exercise continue to work together on this by looking at the list of ideas developed in the first exercise and noting down the information that could be included in their composition.

Step 2. After this step each student individually prepares a summary of the composition which s/he then presents to the others in their group and other members of the group should note down if s/he thought of something they didn't. After that you can offer students the opportunity to present the contents to someone who wrote about the other topic and to hear his/her ideas. In doing so, students are encouraged to give each other additional ideas.

Step 3. The three activities (generating ideas, choosing the audience and planning) engage students to think carefully about the rhetorical problem without having to reduce it to 'completing the task'. The activities of generating ideas and defining the audience focus on planning and highlight the decisions needed to generate and organize ideas.

Step 4. Once the preparatory work is completed, writing should begin, that is, the composing of the text. Previous activities set the stage, and the next activity is transcribing, putting thoughts on paper, and reviewing.

Composing
Step 1. Have the outline and the list of ideas ready while students are writing the text to the selected reader/s. Suggestion: write the initial version of the text and leave it for a couple of days. Don't even think about it, and don't read it. Two days later, take it and read it and answer these two questions:

- Content: Are the ideas you have included still the ones you want to have in the composition?
- Organization: Does the order in which the ideas are presented help convey the message to the reader/s?

If you answered 'no' to any question, rewrite some parts of the composition.

Step 2. When you consider your essay to be good enough, review the language used:
- Verbs: are forms, spelling and accent correct?
- Adjectives: what noun do they go with? Are they appropriate?
- Other elements of language you want your students to focus on.

Activity 7.2 Composing-oriented activity

Conclusion

Developing writing is a key component in developing learners' ability to communicate in a second language. We have presented a composing-oriented approach (Lee and VanPatten, 1995, 2003) which has challenged the way written tasks are practised in a traditional approach. This composing-oriented approach takes into account the various cognitive processes responsible for developing writing skills. Likewise, as with the listening and reading tasks in previous chapters, a similar step-by step approach (pre-writing to writing) is proposed. Developing effective writing tasks should adhere to the following principles:

- defining the rhetorical problem (goal/purpose and audience);
- planning (generating ideas, organizing them, setting goals);
- reviewing (evaluation and review).

Composing-oriented tasks can enhance writing skills, and provide L2 learners with various options about the content of their written compositions.

Suggested Reading

Lee, J., and VanPatten, B. (1995). *Making Communicative Language Teaching Happen*. New York: McGraw-Hill.

Chapter eleven of this volume explores second language writing with the aim of developing written tasks to make L2 learners better writers. The authors adopt a cognitive-process theory of writing to propose a composing-oriented approach to teaching and developing writing skills.

Williams, J. (2005). *Teaching Writing in Second and Foreign Language Classrooms*. New York: McGraw-Hill.

This volume provides an analysis of various theoretical and practical issues in developing foreign language writing abilities. The author offers a series of principles and guidelines for developing effective writing tasks.

8 Key Questions in Second Language Teaching:
Implementing Principles of Learning

Chapter Preview

This chapter provides possible answers to some of the key questions learners and language instructors continually raise about second language learning and teaching.

The questions and answers provided in this chapter deal with many aspects of second language teaching: from the teaching of grammar and correction of errors to the use of effective tasks to develop language skills.

Introduction

In the previous chapters of this book some of the key issues in second language teaching have been covered. In addition to that, concrete examples on how to teach grammar, correct errors, develop language tasks, create conditions for interaction, and provide L2 learners with comprehensible and meaningful input have been offered. After reading this book, readers will still have many issues that they would like to raise which have not been covered and/or for which they request some clarification.

In order to summarize the issues and the topics illustrated in this book, a number of questions about language learning and second language teaching that teachers often ask themselves have been formulated. The questions and answers raised in this section should provide readers with an insight into the best practice in second language teaching.

Key Questions

Are particular types of grammar instruction better than others?

There has been a dramatic shift from traditional grammar-oriented methods to more communicative grammar approaches. This shift has meant a change in the way grammar is taught and practised in the language classroom. In traditional methods, grammar was provided through long and elaborated explanations of the grammatical rules of the target language. Paradigms of those grammatical rules were provided and followed by output-based practice (written and oral exercises) where the main focus was to practise the grammatical rules to obtain accuracy. Traditional grammar instruction practice is usually provided following a particular sequence which goes from mechanical to communicative drills practice. Most books used in the UK and across Europe to teach foreign languages approach the teaching of grammar in a very traditional way. The grammar sections of these books are generally characterized by paradigmatic explanations of linguistic structures and grammatical principles for L1 learners. The paradigmatic explanation is followed by pattern practice and substitution drills. Real-life situations are completely ignored and practice is implemented in a completely decontextualized way. This is not the way we acquire a second language and imitation and repetition play a very small role in SLA (language chunks play a role in second language acquisition; see Myles, Mitchell and Hooper, 1999). Research in SLA has also shown that traditional approaches to grammar instruction which involve the use of drills DO NOT foster acquisition.

The question addressed here is whether there are certain types of grammar instruction better than others, and whether they could be incorporated successfully in the teaching of a second language. The question is not whether or not we should teach grammar, but rather how and what we should teach.

First of all, we must emphasize that the theoretical and empirical findings in second language research have on the one hand indicated the limited role for grammar instruction (e.g. instruction cannot alter the route of acquisition), and on the other hand highlighted the importance of incorporating grammar in a more communicative framework of language teaching by devising grammar tasks that enhance the grammatical features in the input. The question is to determine what type of grammar is more successful in terms of helping learners internalize the grammatical features of a target language. Learners bring to the task of acquisition a variety of internal mechanisms and traits which effectively override most instructional efforts. However, the more researchers learn about what learners do with input and how they do it, the closer they come to understanding the possibilities of instructional effects. Such research insights have driven researchers to examine the effects not of instruction more generally, but of particular kinds of instructional interventions; those that were both input-oriented and meaning-based (see Nassanji and Fotos, 2011 for a full review). These interventions, which aim at manipulating the input L2 learners receive, include approaches such as text enhancement, processing instruction, input flood, consciousness raising, and others (see Chapter 2 of the present book).

When selecting the types of grammar instruction techniques we should take into consideration the nature of the target form.

Therefore to go back to our original question: Are there types of instruction better than others? We must say that there is not one particular type of grammar instruction approach better than others. However, we must emphasize again that effective types of grammar instruction share a common and essential ingredient: input.

In Chapter 2 of this book we have offered language instructors some of the principles they should use when developing grammar tasks. In order to develop effective grammar tasks, instructors should ensure that input is manipulated to facilitate input processing and grammar acquisition. Learners should be encouraged to make accurate form-meaning mappings. Grammar tasks should focus on both form and meaning and output practice should follow input practice. Finally, we have emphasized the importance of using a variety of grammar tasks and the necessity for language instructors to use an eclectic approach to grammar instruction. One size does not fit all!

Are particular types of error correction better than others?

The role of error correction (corrective feedback in the SLA jargon) in SLA has been widely debated, spawning a great deal of theoretical and empirical research. The role of corrective feedback in SLA is not yet clear. Research on corrective feedback in SLA has attempted to prove that corrective feedback exists, it is usable and it is used, and it is necessary.

Explicit corrective feedback provides learners with a meta-linguistic explanation or explicit error correction. This kind of direct error correction might have a temporary effect (improve performance) but does little good in the long run (it does not cause a change in L2 learners' underlying implicit system).

Implicit corrective feedback indirectly and incidentally informs learners of their non-target-like use of certain linguistic features. Recasts, confirmation checks, clarification requests, repetitions, and even paralinguistic signs such as facial expressions can all constitute indirect correction techniques.

Implicit corrective feedback (e.g. confirmation checks, clarification requests, and recasts) aims at inducing learners to detect a discrepancy between their interlanguage and the target language. For implicit corrective feedback, one fundamental question is: How do such indirect signals help learners recognize a discrepancy? Two hypotheses have been proposed:

(1) implicit feedback offers the opportunity to make a comparison;
(2) the output driven by the feedback can stimulate learners to notice the gap.

The first hypothesis proposes that providing the opportunity to identify contrasts between correct forms (i.e., models) and incorrect forms through implicit corrective feedback (i.e., recasts) may promote learners to notice the gap between their interlanguage and the target language. Recast allows the learner to compare the two forms side by side, so to speak, and to observe the contrast (although in some cases the question is whether or not L2 learners actually notice the recast). The second hypothesis is concerned with output: learners' attempts to reformulate their initial utterances may lead them to notice the gap between their interlanguage and the target language.

Indirect correction techniques can be further classified into two types:

1. Recasts – provide the correct form immediately after learner errors.
2. Repair techniques – (e.g. clarification requests, elicitations) do not provide target-like forms. Instead, they promote learners to repair their errors by themselves by providing a chance to reformulate their previous ill-formed utterances.

The question is: what type of indirect correction can be the most beneficial in language learning and teaching? The answer is that the two main types of indirect error correction do different things. Support for repair suggests that this kind of corrective feedback can assist learners in actively confronting errors in ways that may lead to revisions of their hypotheses about the target language. Support for recast suggests that it might enable learners to be exposed to target forms and elicit repetition, and this repetition may, in turn, enhance salience. Enhanced input may also contribute to the acquisition of new linguistic forms. In addition, as claimed previously, learners may be able to juxtapose incorrect and correct forms through recasts, and eventually notice the gap (see also Chapter 3 in the present book).

In Chapter 3 we provided some principles that language instructors should follow in order to provide learners with effective corrective feedback. When correcting errors, instructors should adopt an eclectic approach considering a series of factors such as the form/structure and the learners' proficiency level. Readiness of learners to overcome certain errors must be taken into account. If L2 learners are not ready to process a certain feature because they have not reached that stage, not even corrective feedback will be helpful (Pienemann, 1998). Effective corrective feedback techniques are the ones that seem to produce student-generated repairs. Language instructors should encourage learners to self-correct and they should provide appropriate cues for the learner to self-repair.

Are particular types of explicit information (providing rules) better than others?

It is my view that this is a very good question as generally teachers believe that learning rules causes the acquisition of a target language. When we look at the way languages are learned we begin to ask ourselves whether or not providing rules helps at all. Second language acquisition requires L2 learners to be exposed to comprehensible and meaningful input (explicit information about a target language is not input for acquisition). Instructed second language acquisition research has shown that learning rules is not what makes the difference. Acquisition is not driven by explicit rules but by interaction with input data. Providing explicit information and giving rules might help in terms of proving L2 learners with the opportunity to monitor their speech to perform certain tasks. However, the internal developing system is built up via the regular channels of acquisition and it is not affected by learning the explicit rules of a target language.

Are particular forms or structures (rules) more difficult to acquire than others?

Again this is a common question asked by learners and language instructors. The answer is that there is not a simple explanation and we need to emphasize that classroom rule learning is not the same as acquisition. Second language acquisition is complex and consists of various processes acting sometimes on different data. If we take the English present tense third-person singular -*s*- it is understood that it is an easy rule to learn explicitly, but at the same time, according to research, a very difficult rule to acquire (see VanPatten, 1996) as L2 learners have shown some difficulty in producing this rule. The explanation is that there are multiple factors that would explain the difficulty in acquiring certain rules. In the case of the present tense third-person singular -*s*- in English a combination of factors including redundancy and the communicative value of this rule and other factors (e.g. strategies used by L2 learners to process words and forms in the input) would make this rule difficult to process and acquire. The best answer to this question is that what makes a rule difficult is the fact that various aspects of acquisition come together to make it difficult.

Are particular types of oral tasks for language teaching better than others?

In this book we have argued that instruction should move from input practice to output practice. Acquisition is intake dependent and instructors would need to provide learners with opportunities in the input they are exposed to, to make correct form-meaning connections. Once learners have hopefully internalized forms and made those form-meaning mappings (through structured input activities or other communicative grammar tasks and not through drills or pattern practice) and the linguistics situation in which the language makes use of these form-meaning connections, we should provide opportunity for L2 learners to use the target language for communicative purposes.

Output is the language produced by learners that has a communicative purpose and it is produced for a specific meaning. Oral communicative practice is in antithesis to traditional oral practice largely used in traditional textbooks. In traditional oral tasks learners are asked to look at some pictures or a dialogue and then perform that dialogue following a specific pattern. Another form of traditional oral task which is normally found in language textbooks is to ask L2 learners to talk about a topic (e.g. describe a friend or a member of your family or talk about your weekend...) without taking into consideration the main principles of the communication act (it involves the expression, interpretation and negotiation of meaning in a given context).

Based on what we have said in Chapter 4, we have developed a series of principles/guidelines that language instructors should follow in developing effective oral tasks. Oral tasks should be designed to allow language instructors and learners to interact with each other. The role of the instructor is to design the oral task and encourage participation and contribution from learners. The learner's role is to share responsibility in interaction and task completion. By providing a series of tasks to complete we encourage learners to take responsibility for generating the information themselves rather than just receiving it. Language instructors should develop oral tasks in which learners are provided with opportunities to speak the target language at all times in a rich environment that contains collaborative work, authentic materials and tasks in which they share knowledge by interacting with each other. The ability to communicate in a second language clearly and efficiently contributes to the overall success in the acquisition of a second language. Therefore, it is crucial that language instructors pay greater attention to the development of speaking skills. Rather than leading learners to pure memorization, they should provide learners with a rich environment where meaningful communication takes place. With this aim in mind, various speaking tasks such as those presented in Chapter 4 (e.g. exchange information tasks, role-plays, information-gap tasks) can greatly contribute to the development of learners' communicative skills necessary in order to acquire a second language (see also García Mayo, 2007; Robinson, 2011).

Are particular types of written tasks better than others?

Writing is a cognitive process that involves a series of sub-processes. Writing is a process where learners explore, consolidate and develop rhetorical objectives. The same definition used for communication is applicable to the written language. We express ourselves both in speaking and in writing. When we write a grocery list, for example, we accomplish an act of communication. Traditional writing tasks do not achieve this.

When designing a writing activity for L2 learners, language teachers should take into consideration the mental processes that comprise the act of communication (cognitive-process theory). In doing so, they encourage learners (via a step-by-step approach to the written task) to work together to generate content, select a purpose, plan and organize the composition (prewriting activities) and eventually review and evaluate (content and form) their composition (see Chapter 7).

Are particular types of reading and comprehension tasks better than others?

Reading/comprehension tasks are also an important component of a communicative classroom. The proposed reading comprehension framework is one of the existing communicative approaches that have challenged the way reading is done in traditional approaches (translation and answering questions). When designing a reading comprehension task we should take into account the processes (e.g. Schema theory; see also Han and Anderson, 2009) responsible for reading comprehension and should develop a step-by-step approach (from pre-reading to assimilation) similar to the one used for writing. The so-called Schema theory suggests that, as learners, our knowledge impacts on how we process and understand new incoming information. The pedagogical implication of the Schema theory is the understanding that reading is an interactive process between readers and texts and readers must associate elements in a text with their pre-reading knowledge.

Reading activities in traditional textbooks consist mainly of two types: translation tasks (read a passage and translate it); and answer questions from a text (a typical task/exercise is: Read the dialogue/text and answer the following questions). Reading should be viewed as 'reading in another language rather than as an exercise in translation'. The fact that language learners do not necessarily have the verbal virtuosity of a native reader means instructors need to use some strategies to help them. The framework presented here takes into consideration the need to guide learners in their comprehension of a text. Developing reading comprehension skills involves the interaction of a variety of knowledge sources. In Chapter 6 we proposed an interactive model to develop L2 learners' reading skills. Specific guidelines have been suggested for second language instructors. Reading comprehension tasks should be developed in order to stimulate learners' motivation and should have specific communicative purposes and goals. A five-stage approach should be followed in designing reading comprehension tasks. The pre-reading stage is to prepare students for reading and activating their background knowledge. The reading stage is to help learners to read the text and scan for specific information or meanings. The text-interaction stage is to gradually bridge the gap between the text and the reader. The post-reading stage is to check and verify learners' comprehension. The personalization stage is to help learners to exploit the communicative function of the text through the use of various tasks (e.g. solve a problem, create a poster, apply main concepts to another context, relate key issues to a different context).

Are particular types of listening comprehension tasks better than others?

One particularly important part of language teaching is to help students to develop the ability to listen for a specific purpose. In order to develop learners' listening skills, instructors should provide some tasks which reflect listening situations occurring outside the classroom. Learners should be guided to the task of listening in terms of what meanings they should expect from the passage. At the same time, learners must be able to take responsibility for extracting the main content/information from the text.

The role of comprehensible input and conversational interaction has assumed greater importance in second language teaching as learners benefit a great deal from exposure to comprehensible input, conversational interaction and opportunities for negotiation of meaning.

Listening is not just a bottom-up process where learners hear sounds and need to decode those sounds from the smaller units to large texts, but it is also a top-down process where learners reconstruct the original meaning of the speaker using incoming sounds as clues. In this reconstruction process, the listener uses prior knowledge of the context and situation within which the listening takes place to make sense of what he or she hears. Listeners use a series of mental processes and prior knowledge sources to understand and interpret what they hear. Listening is a very active skill given that learners are actively engaged in different processes while they are exposed to aural stimuli. We can distinguish between three main processes: perceiving; attending; and assigning meaning.

If we look at listening in the language classroom the two main questions to be asked are: What kind of listening tasks are learners engaged in the classroom? Do they have the opportunity to develop their skills and strategies? The challenge is to develop listening tasks which will stimulate the development of listening skills while equipping learners with listening strategies.

When teachers develop listening tasks (see Chapter 5) they should take the following steps:

1. They should expose listeners to comprehensible input.
2. They should use the target language to conduct business.
3. They should allow learners to nominate topics and structure the discourse. Learners are much more likely to get involved and become active listeners and participants.
4. They should develop a listening task for a specific communicative purpose.
5. They should respond to the learner as a listener, not as an instructor.
6. They should provide some good listening gambits to learners. In addition to simply allowing more opportunities for collaborative listening, instructors can also point out learners' typical listening gambits for signalling non-understanding, confirmation, and so forth.

Based on these principles/guidelines a three-stage approach has been proposed (see also Flowerdew and Miller, 2005).

In the pre-listening stage, language instructors should set the context, create motivation and activate learners' prior knowledge through cooperative learning tasks (e.g. brainstorming, think-pair-share). Pre-listening tasks include vocabulary learning and/or identifying key ideas contained in the upcoming input.

In the while-listening stage, tasks require learners to listen for main ideas to establish the context and to transfer information. Learners are exposed to listening bottom-up tasks (e.g. word-sentence recognition, listening for different morphological endings), top-down tasks (identifying the topic, understanding meaning of sentences) and interactive tasks (e.g. listening to a list and categorizing the words, following directions). The main listening tasks at this stage include guided note taking, completion of a picture or schematic diagram or table.

Finally, in the post-listening stage, learners examine the functional language and infer the meaning of vocabulary (e.g. guess the meaning of unknown vocabulary, analyse the success of communication in the script, brainstorm alternative ways of expression). In the final stage of a listening comprehension task, language learners are given post-listening tasks which involve additional reading, writing, speaking, and interaction activities.

Concluding Remarks

Are particular methods in language teaching better than others?

Language instructors are always interested in finding out what is the best way to teach languages. In the last forty years we have witnessed a variety of methods in language teaching (e.g. Grammar Translation, Natural Approach, Communicative Language Teaching, Task-based Instruction). Language instructors should not look at the 'right method' to teach languages, as there isn't one. Practitioners should instead talk about principled and evidence-based approach to language teaching which should be drawn from principles, theories and research in second language acquisition, language use and communication. Language instructors are encouraged to take suggestions from here and there when it comes to pedagogical issues, as long as what they choose is guided and informed by theory and empirical research in language learning and teaching. In this book, it has been argued for a learner-centred type of instruction, where L2 learners engage in communicative and effective tasks which involve group work and interaction with other learners. A teaching environment in which learners are exposed to tasks for a specific purpose and where the instructor is in a position to give students many opportunities for spontaneous production, interaction and negotiation of meaning, and a language classroom where learners receive comprehensible input and are given opportunities to interact with their peers, should be achieved. A different role for the language instructor has been proposed, one that creates the opportunity and the conditions in the classroom for L2 learners to co-participate and take responsibility for their learning. In this new environment learning can take place naturally and teaching can be effective. In this teaching and learning environment, meaning is emphasized over form, and the amount of correction is kept to a minimum, letting the students express themselves and self-repair. Comprehensible, simplified and message-based input is provided through the use of contextual props, cues and gestures rather than structural grading, and a variety of task discourse types introduced by role-playing, stories and authentic materials. L2 learners are exposed to tasks in which they engage in the interpretation, expression and negotiation of meaning.

Based on our discussion in this book a principled and evidence-based approach to second language teaching is proposed. The main tenets of this approach are:

1. Ensure that learners develop linguistics and communicative competence.
2. Ensure that learners engage with language tasks where meaning is emphasized over form. However, a focus on form is an essential component in second language teaching and learning.
3. Ensure that learners are exposed to extensive 'good quality' input. However, it is essential that learners are given opportunities for output.
4. Ensure that learners are exposed to language tasks (e.g. jigsaw tasks, information-gap tasks, problem-solving tasks) where they have the opportunity to interact with each other, exchange information, negotiate meaning, and develop overall fluency skills.
5. Ensure that learners engage in effective tasks (e.g. information-exchange tasks, discourse type tasks, role-playing, real-life materials).
6. Ensure that the amount of error correction is kept to a minimum, and learners are encouraged to self-repair.
7. Ensure that learners have considerable exposure to second language speech from the instructor and other learners and instructors should provide opportunities for learners to play an active role during the language task.
8. Ensure that learners work in pairs or in groups during the completion of a language task. In group work learners are encouraged to negotiate meaning and use a variety of linguistic forms and functions.
9. Ensure that learners engage in language tasks which integrate their skills to reflect a more authentic use of language.
10. Ensure that learners are exposed to authentic materials so that they will be better prepared to deal with real language outside the classroom setting.

Bibliography

Anderson, N. (1999). *Exploring Second Language Reading: Issues and Strategies.* Boston, MA: Heinle and Heinle.

Bacham, L. F., and Palmer, A. S. (1996). *Language Testing in Practice.* Oxford: Oxford University Press.

Benati, A., and Lee, J. F. (2008). *Grammar Acquisition and Processing Instruction: Secondary and Cumulative Effects.* Clevedon: Multilingual Matters.

Benati, A., and Lee, J. F. (2010). *Processing Instruction and Discourse.* London: Continuum.

Bernhardt, E. (1991). *Reading Development in a Second Language.* Norwood, NJ: Ablex.

Brantmeier, C. (ed.) (2009). *Crossing Languages and Research Methods: Analyses of Adult Foreign Language Reading.* Greenwich, CT: Information Age Publishing.

Breen, M., and Candlin, C. (1980). The essentials of a communicative curriculum in language teaching. *Applied Linguistics*, 1, 1–47.

Brown, H. D. (2001). *Teaching by Principles.* New York: Longman.

Bygate, M. (1987). *Speaking.* Oxford: Oxford University Press.

Bygate, M. 2001. Spoken language pedagogy. In Kaplan, R. (ed.), *The Oxford Handbook of Applied Linguistics* (pp. 27–38). Oxford: Oxford University Press.

Byrnes, H. (1984). The role of listening comprehension: a theoretical base. *Foreign Language Annals*, 17, 317–29.

Chomsky, N. (1965). *Aspects of the Theory of Syntax.* Cambridge, MA: MIT Press.

Chomsky, N. (1975). *Reflections on Language.* New York: Pantheon Books.

Corder, P. (1967). The significance of learners' errors. *International Review of Applied Linguistics*, 5, 161–69.

Crandall, J., and Tucker, G. R. (1990). Content-based language instruction in second and foreign languages. In Anivan, S. (ed.), *Language Teaching Methodology for the Nineties* (pp. 83–96). Singapore: SAEMEO Regional Language Centre.

De Biase, B., and Kawaguchi, S. (2002). Exploring the typological plausibility of processability theory: language development in Italian second language and Japanese second language. *Second Language Research*, 18, 274–302.

DeKeyser, R. (ed.) (2006). *Practicing in a Second Language. Perspectives from Applied Linguistics and Cognitive Psychology.* New York: Cambridge University Press.

Doughty, C., and Pica, T. (1986). Information gap tasks: Do they facilitate second language acquisition? *TESOL Quarterly*, 20, 305–325.

Doughty, C., and Williams, J. (eds) (1998). *Focus on Form in Classroom Second Language Acquisition.* Cambridge: Cambridge University Press.

Dulay, H. C., and Burt, M. K. (1974). Natural sequences in child second language acquisition. *Language Learning*, 24, 37–53.

Ellis, R. (1990). *Instructed Second Language Acquisition.* Basil: Blackwell.

Ellis, R. (1991). Grammar teaching practice or consciousness raising? In Ellis, R. (ed.), *Second Language Acquisition and Second Language Pedagogy* (pp. 232–41). Clevedon: Multilingual Matters.

Ellis, R. (1994). *The Study of Second Language Acquisition.* Oxford: Oxford University Press.

Ellis, R. (1997). *SLA Research and Language Teaching.* Oxford: Oxford University Press.

Ellis, R. (2003). *Task-Based Language Learning and Teaching.* Oxford: Oxford: Oxford University Press.

Ellis, R. (2009). Corrective feedback and teacher development. *L2 Journal,* 1, 3–18.

Farley, A. (2005). *Structured Input: Grammar Instruction for the Acquisition-Oriented and Language Teaching.* Oxford: Oxford University Press.

Field, J. (2008). *Listening in the Language Classroom.* Cambridge: Cambridge University Press.

Flower, L., and Hayes, J. R. (1981). A cognitive process theory of writing. *College Composition and Communication,* 32, 365–87.

Flowerdew, J., and Miller, L. (2005). *Second Language Listening: Theory and Practice.* Cambridge: Cambridge University Press.

García Mayo, M. P. (ed.). (2007). *Investigating Tasks in Formal Language Learning.* Clevedon: Multilingual Matters.

Gass, S. (1997). *Input, Interaction, and the Second Language Learner.* Mahwah, NJ: Lawrence Erlbaum.

Gass, S. M., and Mackey, A. (2007). Input, interaction and output in second language acquisition. In VanPatten, B. and Williams, J. (eds), *Theories in Second Language Acquisition: An Introduction* (pp. 175–99). Mahwah, NJ: Lawrence Erlbaum Associates.

Gass, S., and Selinker, L. (2008). *Second Language Acquisition: An Introductory Course.* Mahwah, NJ: Lawrence Erlbaum Associates.

Han, Z., and Anderson, N. J. (2009). *Second Language Reading Research and Instruction: Crossing the Boundaries.* Michigan: University of Michigan Press.

Hinkel, E. (ed.) (2005). *Handbook of Research in Second Language Teaching and Learning.* Mahwah, NJ: Lawrence Erlbaum Associates.

Hymes, D. (1972). On communicative competence. In Pride, J.B. and Holmes, J., *Sociolinguistics: Selected Readings* (pp. 269–93). Harmondsworth: Penguin.

Krashen, S. (1982). *Principles and Practice in Second Language Acquisition.* London: Pergamon.

Krashen, S. (2009). The comprehension hypothesis extended. In Piske, T. and Young-Scholten, M. (eds), *Input Matters* (pp. 81–94). Bristol: Multilingual Matters.

Krashen, S., and Terrell, T. (1983). *The Natural Approach: Language Acquisition in the Classroom.* Hayward, CA: Alemany Press.

Larsen-Freeman, D. (2000). *Techniques and Principles in Language Teaching.* Oxford: Oxford University Press.

Lee, J. (2000). *Tasks and Communicating in Language Classrooms.* New York: McGraw-Hill.

Lee, J. F., and Benati, A. (2007a). *Delivering Processing Instruction in Classrooms and Virtual Contexts: Research and Practice.* London: Equinox.

Lee, J. F., and Benati, A. (2007b). *Second Language Processing: An Analysis of Theory, Problems and Possible Solutions.* London: Continuum.

Lee, J., and Benati, A. (2009). *Research and Perspectives on Processing Instruction.* Berlin: Mouton de Gruyter.

Lee, J., and VanPatten, B. (1995). *Making Communicative Language Teaching Happen.* New York: McGraw-Hill.

Lee, J., and VanPatten, B. (2003). *Making Communicative Language Teaching Happen*, 2nd edn. New York: McGraw-Hill.

Littlewood, W. (1981). *Communicative Language Teaching: An Introduction.* Cambridge: Cambridge University Press.

Long, M. (1983). Does second language instruction make a difference? *TESOL Quarterly*, 17, 359–82.

Long, M. (1991). Focus on form: a design feature in language teaching methodology. In De Bot, K. (eds), *Foreign Language Research in Cross-Cultural Perspectives* (pp. 39–52). Amsterdam: John Benjamins.

Long, M. (1996). The role of the linguistic environment in second language acquisition. In Ritchie, W. C. and Bhatia, T. K. (eds), *Handbook of Second Language Acquisition* (pp. 413–68). San Diego: Academic Press.

Long, M. (2007). *Problems in SLA.* Mahwah, NJ: Lawrence Erlbaum Associates.

Long, M., and Robinson, P. (1998). Focus on form: theory, research and practice. In Doughty, C. and Williams, J. (eds), *Focus on Form in Classroom Second Language Acquisition* (pp. 15–41). Cambridge: Cambridge University Press.

Long, M. H., and Doughty, C. J. (eds) (2009). *The Handbook of Language Teaching.* Oxford: Wiley-Blackwell.

Lyster, R., and Ranta, L. (1997). Corrective feedback and learner uptake: Negotiation of form in communicative classrooms. *Studies in Second Language Acquisition*, 19, 37–66.

Met, M. (1999). *Content-Based Instruction: Defining Terms, Making Decisions.* Washington: The National Foreign Language Center.

Myles, F., Mitchell, R., and Hooper, J. (1999). Interrogative chunks in French L2. *Studies in Second Language Acquisition*, 21, 49–80.

Nassaji, H., and Fotos, S. (2011). *Teaching Grammar in Second Language Classrooms.* New York: Routledge.

Norris, J. M., and Ortega, L. (2000). Effectiveness of L2 instruction: A research synthesis and quantitative meta-analysis. *Language Learning*, 50, 417–528.

Nunan, D. (1989). *Designing Tasks for the Communicative Classroom.* New York: Cambridge University Press.

Nunan, D. (2001). *Second Language Teaching and Learning.* Boston, MA: Heinle and Heinle.

Omaggio Hadley, A. (2001). *Teaching Language in Context.* Boston: Heinle and Heinle.

Ortega, L. (2008). *Understanding Second Language Acquisition.* Oxford: Oxford University Press.

Pica, T. (1994). Questions from the classroom: research perspectives. *TESOL Quarterly*, 29, 49–79.

Pica, T., Karng, H.-S., and Sauro, S. (2006). Information gap tasks: Their multiple roles and contributions to interaction research methodology. *Studies in Second Language Acquisition*, 28, 301–338.

Pienemann, M. (1984). Psychological constraints on the teachability of languages. *Second Language Acquisition*, 6, 186–214.

Pienemann, M. (1987). Determining the influence of instruction on L2 speech processing. *Australian Review of Applied Linguistics*, 10, 83–113.

Pienemann, M. (1998). *Language Processing and L2 Development*. New York: Benjamins.

Richards, J. C. (1990). *The Language Teaching Matrix*. New York: Cambridge University Press.

Richards, J. C., and Rodgers, T. S. (2001). *Approaches and Methods in Language Teaching*. Cambridge: Cambridge University Press.

Robinson, P. (ed.). (2011). *Second Language Task Complexity: Researching the Cognition Hypothesis of Language Learning and Performance*. Amsterdam: John Benjamins.

Rost, M. (1990). *Listening in Language Learning*. London: Longman.

Rost, M. (2002). *Teaching and Researching Listening*. London: Longman.

Rost, M., and Fuchs, M. (2002). *Longman English Interactive, Level 3*. New York: Longman.

Rumelhart, D. (1980). Schemata: the building blocks of cognition. In Bruce, S. B. and Brewer, W. (eds), *Theoretical Issues in Reading Comprehension* (pp. 38–58). Hillsdale, NJ: Lawrence Erlbaum Associates.

Rutherford, W. (1987). *Second Language Grammar: Teaching and Learning*. London: Longman.

Rutherford, W., and Sharwood-Smith, M. (1988). *Grammar and Second Language Teaching*. Rowley, MA: Newbury House.

Savignon, S. (2005). *Communicative Competence: Theory and Classroom Practice*. New York: McGraw-Hill.

Schmidt, R. (1990). The role of consciousness in second language learning. *Applied Linguistics*, 11, 129–58.

Selinker, L. (1972). Interlanguage. *International Review of Applied Linguistics*, 10, 209–231.

Sharwood-Smith, M. (1991). Speaking to many minds: on the relevance of different types of language information for the L2 learner. *Second Language Research*, 7, 118–32.

Sharwood-Smith, M. (1993). Input enhancement in instructed SLA: theoretical bases. *Studies in Second Language Acquisition*, 15, 165–79.

Sheen, Y. (2011). *Corrective Feedback, Individual Differences and Second Language Learning*. New York: Springer.

Skehan, P. (1996). A framework for the implementation of task-based instruction. *Applied Linguistics*, 17, 38–62.

Skinner, B. F. (1957). *Verbal Behavior*. New York: Appleton-Century-Crofts.

Spada, N. (1997). Form-focused instruction and second language acquisition: a review of classroom and laboratory research. *Language Teaching*, 30, 73–87.

Spada, N., and Lightbown, P. (1993) *How Languages are Learned*. Oxford: Oxford University Press.

Storch, N. (2002). Patterns of interaction in ESL pair work. *Language Learning*, 52, 119–58.

Storch, N. (2003). Relationships formed in dyadic interaction and opportunity for learning. *International Journal of Educational Research*, 37, 305–322.

Storch, N. (2007). Investigating the merits of pair work on a text editing task in ESL classes. *Language Teaching Research*, 11, 143–59.

Storch, N. (2008). Metatalk in a pair work activity: level of engagement and implications for language development. *Language Awareness*, 17, 95–114.

Swain, M. (1985). Communicative competence: some roles of comprehensible input and comprehensible output in its development. In Gass, S. and Madden, C. (eds), *Input in Second Language Acquisition* (pp. 235–53). Rowley, MA: Newbury House.

Swain, M. (1995). Three functions of output in second language learning. In Cook, G. and Seidlhofer, B. (eds), *Principles and Practice in the Study of Language* (pp. 125–44). Oxford: Oxford University Press.

Ur, P. (1981). *Discussions that Work*. Cambridge: Cambridge University Press.

Vandergrift, L. (2002). It was nice to see that our predictions were right: developing metacognition in L2 listening comprehension. *Canadian Modern Language Review*, 58, 555–75.

VanPatten, B. (1996). *Input Processing and Grammar Instruction: Theory and Research*. Norwood, NJ: Ablex.

VanPatten, B. (2002). Processing instruction: an update. *Language Learning*, 52, 755–803.

VanPatten, B. (2003). *From Input to Output: A Teacher's Guide to Second Language Acquisition*. New York: McGraw-Hill.

VanPatten, B. (ed.). (2004). *Processing Instruction: Theory, Research, and Commentary*. Mahwah, NJ: Erlbaum.

VanPatten, B., and Sanz, C. (1995). From input to output: processing instruction and communicative tasks. In Eckman, F. R., Highland, D., Lee, P. W., Mileham, J., and Weber, R. R. (eds), *Second Language Acquisition Theory and Pedagogy* (pp. 169–85). Mahwah, NJ: Erlbaum.

VanPatten, B., and Williams, J. (eds) (2007) *Theories in Second Language Acquisition*. Mahwah, NJ: Erlbaum.

VanPatten, B., and Benati, A. (2010). *Key Terms in Second Language Acquisition*. London: Continuum.

VanPatten, B., and Jegerski, J. (2010). *Research in Second Language Processing and Parsing*. Amsterdam: John Benjamins.

Wajnryb, R. (1990). *Grammar Dictation*. Oxford: Oxford University Press.

Wenden, A. (1998). Metacognitive knowledge and language learning. *Applied Linguistics*, 19, 515–37.

White, L. (2003). *Second Language Acquisition and Universal Grammar*. Cambridge: Cambridge University Press.

Williams, J. (2005). *Teaching Writing in Second and Foreign Language Classrooms*. New Jersey: McGraw-Hill.

Wolvin, A., and Coakley, C. (1995). *Listening*. New Jersey: McGraw-Hill.

Wong, W. (2004). The nature of processing instruction. In VanPatten, B. (ed.), *Processing Instruction: Theory, Research, and Commentary* (pp. 33–63). Mahwah, NJ: Erlbaum.

Wong, W. (2005). *Input Enhancement: From Theory and Research to the Classroom*. New York: McGraw-Hill.

Wong, W., and VanPatten, B. (2003). The evidence is IN: Drills are OUT. *Foreign Language Annals*, 36, 403–423.

Zhang, M. (2000). *Step by Step 2*. Shanghai: East China Normal University Publishing House.

Key Terms

Clarification request/confirmation check

The two terms refer to a series of conversational and interaction devices used by both learners and instructors to require more information when there is a breakdown in communication. Learners and instructors sometimes request clarifications (e.g. what did you say?) and/or confirmations (e.g. did you say…) if they do not comprehend language input. Both devices are an alternative way to provide L2 learners with corrective feedback. The debate as to whether and to what clarification request and confirmation check techniques contribute to second language acquisition is still very much an open one. Many scholars (e.g. Susan Gass, Michael Long, Alison Mackey) in second language acquisition have indicated that conversational interaction and negotiation can facilitate acquisition by making linguistics features more salient to the learner. A variety of empirical studies have investigated the beneficial effects of these devices and the main findings have overall confirmed their positive effects at helping the development of learners' grammatical competence.

Comprehensible input

This term refers to simplified and modified input that learners need in order to acquire a second language. According to Stephen Krashen, input is an effective tool for acquisition (see also **Input**), if it contains a message that can be comprehended by L2 learners. Features in language (e.g. vocabulary, grammar, pronunciation) make their way into the learner's language system only if they are linked to some kind of meaning and are comprehensible to L2 learners. Simplified input is easier to process (e.g. simpler syntax reduces the burden of language processing) and it would also enhance the ability for learners to link one form to one meaning. Use of non-linguistic means, familiar items and concrete tasks make input more comprehensible in the language classroom.

Consciousness raising

This term refers to a particular approach to grammar teaching which intends to raise learners' consciousness on a specific grammatical form/structure in a targeted L2. It is in line with the view that education is a process of discovery through problem-solving tasks. Making certain features salient in the input might help to draw learners' attention to those specific features (Michael Sharwood-Smith, Rod Ellis). The main goal of the consciousness raising approach is to make learners conscious of the rules that govern the use of particular language forms while providing the opportunity to engage in meaningful interaction. Consciousness raising tasks can be inductive or deductive. In the case of an inductive task learners are provided with some language data and are required to provide an explicit representation of the target linguistic feature. In the case of a deductive task learners are given a description of the target linguistic feature and are required to use that description to apply it to L2 data.

In order to develop effective consciousness raising tasks we must adhere to the following guidelines: the task must focus on a form/structure that is a source of difficulty for language learners; the language data provided are adequate to make learners discover the rule; the task provides learners with an opportunity for applying the rule to construct a personal statement in order to promote its storage as explicit knowledge.

Corrective feedback

This term refers to a series of techniques (see also **Recast**) that involves drawing learners' attention to an error in their input. The interest in the role of feedback on errors is partly related to the fact that exposure to comprehensible input is a necessary ingredient for acquisition but might not be sufficient. Corrective feedback techniques are used by instructors to provide feedback to L2 learners about the incorrectness of utterances. Metalinguistic feedback is a corrective feedback technique where non-native speakers are provided with a metalinguistic cue in the input and/or metalinguistic feedback about the correctness of an utterance. Direct elicitation is another form of corrective feedback in the attempt to elicit the correct form from the learner by repeating the learner's utterance. The debate as to whether and to what extent these techniques are effective and contribute to second language acquisition is still an open one.

Dictogloss

This term refers to a collaborative output task which aims at helping L2 learners to elicit output and use their grammar resources to reconstruct a text. Hossein Nassaji and Sandra Fotos have argued that dictogloss tasks are designed to draw learners' attention to language forms/structures while promoting negotiation of meaning. It is a technique which consists of four stages: preparation; dictation; reconstruction; and analysis with correction. In the first stage, learners are given information about the passage that they will be hearing through discussions of the topic and vocabulary. In the second stage, the instructor dictates the passage and learners listen to the passage and take notes of key words. In the third stage, learners are arranged in small groups and, using their notes, they reconstruct the text. In the final stage, learners analyse and correct their work. Reconstruction cloze is a collaborative task similar to a dictogloss task. The only difference is that L2 learners are provided with a cloze task and are required to supply missing items (e.g. target forms/structures).

Exchange information tasks
This term refers to pedagogical tasks where L2 learners engage in oral communication and use the information they have gathered to accomplish a task. James Lee and Bill VanPatten have provided the following guidelines to develop these types of activities: identification of a topic; design an appropriate and immediate purpose; identify the information source.

Focus on form
This term refers to any pedagogical attempts to draw learners' attention to linguistic properties of a target second language. When acquiring a second language, learners follow developmental sequences (Manfred Pienemann), learn morphemes in a similar order (Stephen Krashen), have access to innate knowledge (Lydia White), and analyse and process linguistic input (Bill Van Patten). Although exposure to input is a crucial factor in second language acquisition, it is also true that drawing learners' attention to the formal properties of a L2 language within a meaningful context (focus on form) might have a facilitative role in helping learners to acquire a language more efficiently and more speedily. Catherine Doughty and Jessica Williams have distinguished between reactive and proactive approaches to focus on form. In a proactive approach, a grammar task (see **Consciousness raising, Processing instruction, Input enhancement**) is designed to ensure that there are opportunities to focus, process and use problematic forms while understanding or communicating a message. A reactive approach instead involves the use of a technique (see **Recast**) for drawing learners' attention to errors.

Input
This term refers to the language learners hear or read. Many scholars (e.g. Susan Gass, Nick Ellis, Bill VanPatten) have agreed that input is the main ingredient for the acquisition of a second language. Two main characteristics make input useful for the learner: input must be message-oriented; input must be comprehensible. Input must contain a message that learners must attend to. Input must also be comprehended by the learner if acquisition is to happen.

Input enhancement

This term refers to a particular pedagogical intervention which attempts to bring a particular form/structure to L2 learners' focal attention by enhancing the input through the use of various devices such as textual enhancement. In textual enhancement activities the target form is enhanced visually, altering its appearance in the text (i.e. the form can be italicized, bolded, visually altered with a different colour or underlined). The form/structure is highlighted in a text/dialogue with the hope that learners will notice it.

Input flood

This term refers to a pedagogical intervention where L2 learners are exposed to many instances of the same form/structure in the input. The form is not usually highlighted and the instructor does not draw learners' attention to it. Input flood is a type of intervention that merely saturates the input with the form/structure.

The purpose of designing/using input flood activities is to help learners to be exposed to a greater amount of input containing the target form which hopefully will allow learners to notice and subsequently acquire this form.

Jigsaw task

This term refers to a collaborative output task where L2 learners can work in pairs or in small groups. Each pairs or groups have different information and have to exchange their information to complete the task. Each individual or pairs must give and receive information and therefore opportunities for negotiation of meaning are promoted during jigsaw tasks. The puzzle pieces take various forms (photo, sentence, tape recording, for example).

Negotiation of meaning

This term refers to interactional modifications such as comprehension checks or requests for clarification between an instructor and a learner or between a learner and another learner during communication. Negotiation of meaning is triggered when there is a communication breakdown between two or more interlocutors. The purpose of negotiation is to resolve the communication breakdown and can occur in just about any kind of interaction.

Output

This term refers to the language that learners produce. Merrill Swain has argued that language production (oral and written) can help learners to generate new knowledge and consolidate or modify their existing knowledge. Swain assigns several roles for output: output practice helps learners to improve fluency; output practice helps learners to check comprehension and linguistic correctness; output practice helps learners to focus on form; output helps learners to realize that the developing system is faulty and therefore notice a gap in their system. Swain has pointed out that comprehensible input might not be sufficient to develop native-like grammatical competence and learners also need comprehensible output. L2 learners need 'pushed output', that is speech or writing that will force learners to produce language correctly, precisely and appropriately.

Processing instruction

This term refers to a type of focus on form whose main aim is to help L2 learners to accurately and appropriately process grammatical forms/structures in the input. It is a type of focus on form which draws on the principles of the input processing model developed by Bill VanPatten. This new pedagogical approach seeks to intervene in the processes learners use to get data from the input. Research on input processing has attempted to describe what linguistic data learners attend to during comprehension and which ones they do not attend to, for example what grammatical roles learners assign to nouns or how the position in an utterance influences what gets processed. These processing principles seem to provide an explanation of what learners are doing with input when they are asked to comprehend it. As a result of the way learners attend to input data, Bill VanPatten has developed a pedagogical model called processing instruction which guides and focuses learners' attention when they process input. Processing instruction is a more effective method for enhancing language acquisition as it is used to ensure that learners' focal attention during processing is directed towards the relevant grammatical items and not elsewhere in the sentence. Its main objective is to help learners to circumvent the strategies used by them to derive intake data by making them rely exclusively on form and structure to derive meaning from input. Processing instruction consists of three main components: learners are given explicit information about a linguistic structure or form; learners are given information on a particular processing principle that may negatively affect their picking up of the form or structure during comprehension; learners are pushed to process the form or structure during structured input activities in which the input is manipulated in particular ways to push learners to become dependent on form to get meaning. Structured input activities can be of two types: referential and affective.

Recast

This term refers to a type of corrective feedback in which language instructors provide a correct version of an incorrect utterance. Recasts are restatements of a learner's utterance that occur naturally in interactions. They usually occur when the L2 learners have produced some kind of non-native-like utterance and the other interlocutor is confirming what the learner intended to say, as a kind of confirmation check (see also **Confirmation check**).

Role-play

This term refers to a pedagogical task in which learners engage in real communication in a specific social and cultural context. It is a teaching technique which requires several steps: choose a situation and set the story; provide learners with information, vocabulary and roles; have learners performing the role-play task; allow flexibility for learners to modify the role-play situation; provide feedback.

Structured output task

This term refers to a type of form-focused task which involves the exchange of previously unknown information and requires learners to access a particular form of structure to express meaning. James Lee and Bill VanPatten have provided some guidelines to develop structured input activities: present one thing at a time; keep meaning in focus; move from sentences to connected discourse; use both written and oral output; others must respond to the content of the output.

Index